T0285689

BOOKSHOP DOGS

From the author of
The Bookseller at the End of the World

BOOKSHOP DOGS

RUTH SHAW

ALLEN&UNWIN
SYDNEY•MELBOURNE•AUCKLAND•LONDON

First published in 2023

Text © Ruth Shaw, 2023

Allen & Unwin
Level 2, 10 College Hill, Freemans Bay
Auckland 1011, New Zealand
Phone: (64 9) 377 3800
Email: auckland@allenandunwin.com
Web: www.allenandunwin.co.nz

83 Alexander Street
Crows Nest NSW 2065, Australia
Phone: (61 2) 8425 0100

A catalogue record for this book is available from the National Library of New Zealand.

ISBN 978 1 99100 626 4

Design by Saskia Nicol
Illustrations and handwritten font by Sophie Watson
Photography by Graham Dainty
Set in Feijoa
Printed in China by 1010 Printing Limited

10 9 8 7 6 5 4 3 2

For my dear sister Jill,
who has the capacity to love
every dog and cat
that crosses her path.

CONTENTS

AUTHOR'S NOTE

So many dogs come to my bookshops and that gave me the idea to write about them. Many books have been written about dogs, such as *Quake Dogs* by Laura Sessions, *How to Walk a Dog* by Mike White and *Good Dogs Don't Make it to the South Pole* by Hans-Olav Thyvold. These are just three must-reads. Bookshops also often feature in great books; I have five books on my bookshelf about bookshops, so why not a combination of the two?

This book is very different from my first book, *The Bookseller at the End of the World*. Thankfully it was a much easier book to write, and there were not so many tears. Dogs are gracious, willing, patient, loyal, entertaining and so much more. They are often the colour of our days. Today I am sad, today I am happy, today I want only your love. I sincerely hope you enjoy reading this book as much as I loved writing it.

Ruth

PREFACE

Our family was a 'cat family'. Throughout my childhood, and up until I left home to join the navy, we were never without a cat — or two.

It wasn't until I was discharged from the Royal New Zealand Navy at the age of 20 that a friend gave me my first dog, a medium-sized German shepherd named Rewa. She was everything I wasn't: uncomplicated and laid-back. She travelled with me from Auckland to Stewart Island in my wee 1946 Ford Prefect, sitting in the front seat, eagerly watching the countryside slip by as we headed south. But when I left Stewart Island, Rewa stayed behind as she had attached herself to Mum and Dad, who led the type of lifestyle she was searching for.

My next dog was Buka, a small mongrel, more the shape of a piglet, covered in an array of blotchy browns, with a button black nose, dark brown eyes and a stiff stick-like tail. I was 29 by now, living on a small farmlet up in New South Wales on the New England Tablelands with my husband Tony. Buka was eager to please and he clearly needed a playmate — he was having trouble encouraging our grumpy pregnant sow, Horrible Howard, to play with him. We visited the pound and picked up Jericho, a medium-sized golden all-sort with whiskers around her face and eyes, soft pointed ears, and a tail that obviously belonged to a golden retriever.

Jericho, soon shortened to Jerry, was my constant companion, and my rock when it came to surviving an abusive marriage. When I finally left Tony after four years, Jerry came with me, and together we sailed the east coast of Australia in my 30-foot sailboat *Magic*. (These and other episodes in my rather eventful life are described in my recent book *The Bookseller at the End of the World*.) Like all good boat dogs, Jerry loved fresh fish. Nothing fazed her: she slept through storms curled up in the pile of sails by the chain locker; she never urinated below deck but always near a side stay, and when she urgently needed to poo she went on the coil of rope near the base of the mast.

Jerry was adopted by a friend in Coffs Harbour when she became pregnant to his handsome blue heeler named Banjo. She was totally devoted to Banjo and would often just sit beside him gazing at him in adoration. I am certain she knew I was leaving.

When I hugged her goodbye she licked the tears off my cheeks and looked me straight in the eye as if to say, 'Thanks for all the fish!' Tail wagging vigorously, she turned and ran over to join her hunky, handsome Banjo.

Hunza

INTRODUCING HUNZA

Four years later I came home to New Zealand to live with Lance in Manapōuri, and was employed by the Invercargill City Council as a detached youth worker, the word 'detached' being a clue to the freedom I had. I wasn't answerable to anyone except a committee that required regular reports. Apart from that, I was free to work with youth without being controlled by Social Welfare or the police. After just a few months I knew I needed — and wanted — a dog. Not just as a companion for me — I strongly believed that many of the young people I worked with needed a pet, an animal they could love and that would love them back unconditionally.

Lance and I travelled up to Christchurch and started to look for a German shepherd — not a puppy but a dog past the shoe-chewing stage and yet still young enough to train. A dog I could rely on. After we had seen a number of dogs, Lance decided that it would be better if he continued the search by himself, as I fell in love with every one we saw. 'OH! How *gorgeous* is this dog?! Look, Lance, he wants to come home with us. How can we *not* take this dog home?!'

Totally focused on finding the right dog for me, Lance dropped me off at my aunty and uncle's place and headed off to check out the last few hopefuls left on our list. He returned with a small, shorthaired German shepherd that looked terrified in the back of the car. Ears down, eyes wide and a big question mark on his beautiful face. He was the runt of the litter and no one really wanted him. I was in love straight away. *I wanted him.*

Lance had found him through Dogwatch Adoption and had the signed official paperwork to prove that he was now ours. His name was Sam and he was 12 months old. The assessment read: *Sam is still at the playful stage. Has ok disposition and learns very quickly. Has adjusted very quickly to his new environment.*

Then, under Special Care, it read: *Sam needs firm and loving handling. Plenty of exercise and to be able to run free in a well-fenced yard. Still at the chewing stage so old shoes or rubber bone should be provided. Needs to be watched with washing on the line.*

Lance was asked why we wanted him, so the following was recorded under Requirement: *Companion and guard dog for detached youth worker in Invercargill.* Total cost: a donation of $10. Over the nine-hour drive from Christchurch to Manapōuri I constantly talked to my new dog, hugging him closely. I really was smitten.

I renamed him Hunza.

Why Hunza? When I became a vegetarian, I read about the people who live in the Hunza Valley, a mountainous valley in the foothills of the Himalayas. They were thought to be the happiest and healthiest people in the world, and with no cases of cancer. Some put this down to their consumption of vitamin B-17, also known as amygdalin, found in apricot seeds. The Hunza diet consisted largely of raw fruits and vegetables, with very little meat. I myself often ate Hunza pie, which is easy to make and wonderful for vegetarians as it is full of vitamins and minerals.

On the next page you will find a recipe for this delicious pie.

Hunza pie

1 kg potatoes
big bunch spinach or silverbeet, chopped
1 teaspoon salt
1 teaspoon kelp
2 tablespoons vegetable oil
any pastry shell
handful grated cheese (optional)

Boil the potatoes. Mash them and add the chopped
spinach, salt, kelp and oil. Spoon into the pie crust, top
with cheese if using and bake for 45 minutes at 180°C.

It was the start of an amazing relationship. Hunza was loved by many, becoming the most famous (and infamous dog) in Invercargill. He had so much love to give, and was always up for action. At this time Lance worked 10 days a time at sea, skippering the Department of Conservation's vessel the *Renown* on the Fiordland coast. This was followed by five days at home. To work in with his schedule I rented a flat in Invercargill and worked 10 days straight, then took five days off to coincide with his break. It was a system that suited us both.

In my youth worker position I was given a Toyota Hiace van to drive, which was great as I could load up to eight kids plus Hunza in the back. The van was plain white and I reckoned it needed something painted on it so everyone could easily recognise it. I spoke to one of the tutors at the Salvation Army's work experience programme and he assured me that the 'boys' in his workshop could come up with something. I left the van with him.

Five days later he rang to say the van was ready. Parked in the middle of the workshop was my exceptionally clean van with a massive, colourful zip painted over where the sliding door opened and up over the roof. It was stunning. When you opened the side door the zip opened; when you closed it the zip closed. My van was now certainly recognisable.

I was working with young people aged between nine and 20. Initially, to get my name known, I spent time speaking at schools, working the streets at night, mixing with the gangs and speaking to groups like Lions, Women's Institute, church groups, and to teams of police and Social Welfare staff. Although I had a small office on the second floor above some shops in the main street, my main place of work was in the van with Hunza.

In a very short time we were known everywhere and my office phone was constantly ringing. Cellphones were not even heard of back then, so I had an answerphone that was constantly busy. If Hunza wasn't with me, in my office, he was in the van parked in the main street, which was never locked. Kids just hopped in to hang out with him. When I looked out my office window I could see Hunza surrounded by a bunch of adoring fans.

One small Māori boy would often be waiting for me in the van, curled up beside Hunza who laid quietly alongside him, alert and on guard. I eventually got to know the nine-year-old — although he didn't talk to me, he talked constantly to Hunza. Often as I drove him home I would listen as he confided in Hunza, sharing his innermost secrets. When we arrived at his house he would reluctantly get out and without a word walk slowly up the drive. I was very concerned about the boy but I had to be patient and wait until he was ready to speak to me.

After a few weeks when I was driving him home, I overheard him saying softly, 'Hunza, want to come with me? We can look after each other. Do you think you could chase my father away? I know you could.'

There was a silence as he hugged my dog.

I stopped the van and climbed into the back, sitting opposite them. 'You can't take Hunza home, sweetheart, but maybe between us we can do something.'

He shook his head as he tried to hide his tears. 'It has to be Hunza, he understands.'

'What does he understand?'

'Everything.'

'What time does your dad get home?' I asked.

'Tea time.' It was just before 5 p.m. so we had a little time before his father arrived. I drove quickly to his house and told him to stay with Hunza in the van while I went to speak to his mother. The door opened even before I knocked. His mother stood in the doorway. Her face was bruised, and when she spoke, I noticed some teeth were broken.

'I'm Ruth. Your wee boy is in the van with my dog, Hunza, He is safe...'

'I know all about Hunza,' she interrupted me. 'Thanks.'

'Pack a couple of bags and I'll take you both to a safe-house. I will help you.'

She stood looking at me with wet, vacant eyes, her arms clasped tightly around her body.

'Please let me help,' I pleaded.

I saw a tiny nod, and she turned and went inside. I followed. We quickly packed bags, grabbing clothes, toys, shoes, even a toothbrush and some makeup. We closed the door behind us and ran to the van. She hugged her wee boy and then grabbed Hunza and wept.

'Thank you, thank you, thank you, you precious dog,' she sobbed.

I spoke to the police, and even though the father tried to get his abused family back, he failed.

This was Hunza's first successful case, and there were many more to come.

TWO WEE BOOKSHOPS AND THE SNUG

M y three bookshops in Manapōuri are now pretty well known, since the publication of *The Bookseller at the End of the World*. People have been turning up in droves. Manapōuri is the westernmost town in New Zealand and borders the Fiordland National Park, with a population of 222.

My vision was one small bookshop, hence the name Wee Bookshop painted on the side of the cottage facing the road. As I have always loved books and book people, the bookshop gave me the opportunity — or excuse — to go out and buy more books. After only a year I had a second, even smaller, bookshop arrive on a trailer, and it sits comfortably opposite the main shop, tucked into the fenceline. It is the Children's Bookshop. As though that wasn't enough, I had a third — tiny — bookshop built around an old English linen cupboard. With its little verandah and bench seat, we call it The Snug. All three are painted bright colours — red, blue, yellow, orange and green — and in spring the flowers in the garden turn the area into something magical. Three beautiful wee spaces crammed with books but offering a lot more — friendship, a safe haven, a place to relax and laugh, or cry.

One morning Lance, my amazing husband, as usual parked our small 1963 Kermit-green Fiat, advertising The Smallest Bookshop in New Zealand, on the main highway. An open sign was placed on the corner of Home Street, and we set up tables in between the shops, stacking them with more books. Within minutes my first customers pulled up in a campervan.

The casually dressed woman was full of smiles. 'So glad you're open,' she said. Her husband had already found the bench seat in The Snug, with its collection of books on tractors, trains, cars, motorbikes, farming, fishing and hunting. I had only just welcomed them when the woman suddenly squealed, 'George! George! Look, there's a book here called WOOF!'

WOOF: A Book of Happiness for Dog Lovers, by Anouska Jones, had only just been put up on the shelf. The woman ran over to the campervan, opened the sliding door and out jumped a little white and brown shorthaired dog. He went straight to the dog tree and peed all around the trunk, a look of relief all over his face. Then he had a quick drink of water before jumping up on the man's knee.

'What is your dog's name?' I asked.

'Woof Woof. I just have to buy this book for him.'

Did I really hear this?

They left with three books — a fishing book for him, a holiday reading book for her, and WOOF for . . . well, yes.

It was right then that I had the idea for this book. So *many* dogs visit the bookshops. There are the local dogs, there are 'holiday dogs', who are lucky enough to have holiday homes in and around Manapōuri, and there are what I call 'travelling dogs'. They arrive with their owners in many different modes of transport — in the backs of cars; on a bed in the back of a campervan; in the backs of SUVs, heads hanging out the window; sometimes proudly perched in front helping with the driving; and even in little trailers with windows, attached to the backs of push bikes, which are now nearly all electric.

Every dog has a story, but in this book I can only include a few, including two very special bookshop dogs, Hunza and Cove.

Shady Lady

SHADY LADY
AND THE
PHOTOGRAPHER

Wherever Graham Dainty goes, there is Shady, his Australian blue heeler. Shady was born into a lineage of high-country working dogs, sought after for their speed and ability to work cattle and other stock. As a pup she become a fiftieth birthday present for a woman on a neighbouring farm near Te Anau. Graham, known to everyone as Dainty, is a tall man who is always dressed in shorts. He is an electrician and just happened to be working on this farm one day when the owner's inquisitive blue heeler started to follow him around.

She was attentive, chilled out and totally confident. Dainty remarked to the owner that she was a great dog and was surprised to be told that Shady was only six months old. 'No way!' replied Dainty. 'Pups are usually nuts at that age.'

The farmer told him that for various reasons they couldn't keep the pup, and they were looking for a new home for her. Like a 16-year-old in love, Dainty was already smitten and couldn't stop thinking about her. A week later she jumped into his work van, settled comfortably on the front seat, and he took her home.

Cattle dog to town dog was always going to be a major lifestyle change. Luckily blue heelers are intelligent dogs, so after a minimal amount of self-re-education, blue heeler became blue collar, a towny working dog. Every day she is out in the van with Dainty, usually quite content to sit and watch as he works on building sites. However, sometimes she ventures out and gets into a little mischief.

All dogs get a bit bored when there's no action for long periods, or when they're not the centre of attention, and Shady is no different. When Dainty is working he will sometimes feel a nudge in the back of the leg. 'Come on, time to play,' Shady's eyes say. Or she'll present him with a scrap of timber for a game of fetch, which is a one-sided affair since she only brings it halfway back. If he ignores her she will find her own fun, which may mean finding a piece of plumbing and giving it a good chew.

Her favourite work sites are rural ones, where there is an opportunity to do a bit of rabbiting or excavation for old bones. She can become a bit engrossed in what she's doing, and if Dainty wants to leave and there's no sign of her, it can take a bit of calling to get Shady trotting back, usually with a grin on her face.

Sometimes on a sunny day she'll sunbathe, lying in the sun flat on her back with all four legs in the air.

Dainty, who mostly reads when he's on holiday or has a bit of down time, likes travel books and books he can learn from. He has always loved reading, visiting libraries and constantly buying books. He has a good selection of photography books, not the ones with just pretty pictures but the heavier technical reads. He can't resist a beautifully crafted photography book, such as Jane Ussher's *Still Life*, the large-format book on Shackleton's and Scott's Antarctic huts, or Michael Kenna's *Hokkaido*, with its maple wood cover and exquisite printing.

Books were his main source of finding information before the internet, but even now you will often find him head down in a book. He is always after learning something new, his reading branching out from photography to musicians and their biographies, books on human endurance and exploration, or epic motorcycle adventures, such as Ted Simon's *Jupiter's Travels*. Beautifully written adventures like Robert Macfarlane's *Underland* and *The Old Ways* have also found their way into his library.

Dainty is president of the Fiordland Camera Club, which was set up about 35 years ago by him, Lance, me and a few other local avid amateur photographers. We were mostly interested in trips away, getting out there and 'doing stuff'. Even though our embryonic club was disorganised, with very loose guidelines, *not rules*, we all travelled down to the monthly meetings of the (very organised) Southland Photographic Society. We delighted in pushing the boundaries, looking for different ways of taking photos, and our small club won many of the society's trophies, much to the dismay of some.

Dainty is a strong supporter of the network of camera clubs run through the Photographic Society of New Zealand, and values the opportunity to learn and to share his knowledge with members as they discuss their photos. Even now, 30-plus years later, the small group from the Fiordland Camera Club still bring home most of the annual trophies.

In 1994 Dainty joined Lance as a crew member on the *Evohe*, the sailing vessel we leased when we first ventured into charter work. His first trip down to the subantarctic Campbell Island was one of his earliest adventures. The rest of the crew were very impressed with his photography but less so with his seamanship — he was seasick for the whole voyage. Nevertheless, he decided seasickness was a small price to pay for an introduction to true wilderness.

Today, Dainty always has his camera bag with him, as he is constantly on the lookout for the money shot. His faithful Shady Lady travels with him everywhere, so all the local tradies know her. Another day, another site, constantly together. Luckily, she has Dainty, a dog owner who believes dogs should be dogs. For Shady, commands are just suggestions. She obeys eventually, but often Dainty can see her waiting after he has given a command, as if weighing her options. Then, when the command is repeated in a sterner tone, she clearly thinks, 'Oh! Okay.'

If I have electrical work to be done around the bookshops, I call Shady and Dainty. It was his beautiful photography, the strength of his relationship with his dog, and his professional but friendly approach that told me I wanted Dainty as the photographer for this book.

HUNZA — STOLEN

ALTHOUGH I WASN'T attached to the police I was constantly at the police station, working together with Bruce, the youth aid officer. He was understanding, fair and extremely supportive of my work. A high percentage of the youth I worked with were 'known to the police'.

I would always tie up Hunza at the front entrance to the police station to wait for me. He was never any trouble, but one afternoon trouble came to him in a big way. Having finished my business with the police I came out of the station and Hunza was gone. There was no sign of his collar or lead. I ran back inside and explained to the duty officer, who didn't seem concerned. 'He'll come back, or he'll go home. Don't worry.'

I drove up and down the streets of Invercargill searching for him — around the parks and school grounds — but he was nowhere to be found. Word spread quickly that Hunza was missing and everyone who knew him was shocked as it became clear that he must have been stolen. The reaction among Hunza's friends was wide-ranging, from anger through to tears — even some of the hardened gang members were there to support me. Local radio reported the news.

'Whoever has Hunza please ring us. Just leave him somewhere where we can pick him up.'

Days went by with no news.

Finally the radio station received an anonymous phone call saying Hunza could be found in an empty house in south Invercargill. The police went and picked him up, dirty and hungry but otherwise healthy. When I went to collect him they said they had the suspect in one of the cells. Apparently one of the guys who had to report to the police each afternoon came across Hunza tied up outside the police station and assumed he was a police dog. He decided to take him home, thinking how impressed his mates would be that he was now the owner of a highly trained police dog.

No doubt his excitement would have quickly turned to frustration when Hunza didn't respond to any of his commands. Hunza was a pacifist. He would sit and walk on command, he was eager to please and would do almost anything you asked, but 'Hold!' and 'Attack!' were not in his vocabulary. After four days of trying to get some kind of aggressive reaction to his commands the guy gave up, realising he didn't have a trained police dog on his hands, he had a lookalike: a German shepherd pet who just wanted to play and please everyone.

The constable handed Hunza back to me with a big smile. 'Ruth, we can deal with this in two ways. You can press charges, or you can leave it up to us to deal with it.'

'You deal with it. I'm just happy to have my dog back.'

'We'll introduce him to a real police dog, that should do it,' the officer replied with an even bigger smile.

Apparently they took a police dog into the man's cell and ordered it to sit still unless the culprit went to move, and then the dog was under orders to 'Hold!' I'm not sure how long this lesson went on for, but I smiled when I thought about the culprit sitting completely still, terrified to move, with a well-trained police dog watching him intently, waiting, just waiting for him to move.

Everyone was happy that Hunza had been found unharmed, and he was eager to get back into the van. With excited whining combined with half-hearted barking, he told me all about his latest adventure.

After a good bath and brush, followed by a big meal, Hunza was back on the job.

Lucky

LUCKY THE PIG DOG

J ust after I opened my first Wee Bookshop, a tall dark-haired man walked in one day, with the confidence of a young farmer or hunter. He was dressed in a tartan Swanndri top, shorts and heavy boots and introduced himself as Dean. Looking through the Fiordland books, he found a book he had been looking for: *Port Preservation* by A.C. Begg and N.C. Begg. As he browsed through it he came across a photo of A.C. Begg's son Charles. It was at this point Dean told me that A.C. Begg was in fact his Great-Uncle Alistair.

This initial visit to my bookshop was the first of many; Dean became a regular, sometimes alone but often with his wife, Sarah, and their three children, Lex, Joe and Flossy. Not only is Dean a great reader but the children also love books so they are regular visitors to the Children's Bookshop.

Dean met Sarah at the Riccarton races in Christchurch, where his dad was racing a horse. Sarah was in her final year at Lincoln University. After a number of years courting

Dean finally found the courage to buy an engagement ring, but it was another 18 months before he actually proposed. Dean and Sarah have a holiday home in Manapōuri, and are the parents of Lex, my Bookshop Assistant, whom you may have already met in my previous book.

Dean discovered a love of reading around the age of seven, starting by reading all his father's Barry Crump books, which were the only books around. He also remembers reading the wonderful *Tat: The Story of a New Zealand Sheep Dog* by Neil McNaughton. Published in 1970, this book tells the story of a South Island sheepdog from puppyhood through to maturity.

Through his high-school years Dean lost interest in reading but rediscovered books in his twenties. He finds reading peaceful and therapeutic; it settles his mind after a day's farming, and he also likes the knowledge he gains, even though he reckons he only retains about 15 per cent of what he reads. When he goes into the bush hunting and fishing he takes a book. 'I would worry if I didn't have a book to read,' he told me. He has books stacked up beside his bed, and he often puts books aside for his boys to read when they're older. He believes reading is in his genes.

Dean is such a prolific reader I often lend him books, and in return he brings me one of his books to read, or he turns up with a large cut of wild pork, even some whitebait, pāua or crayfish all for Lance. We firmly believe I'm on the winning side of this arrangement.

Dean's father's farm, Birchwood Station, has been in the family for a hundred years. It was named in 1867 by Captain James Gardener, who was renowned for his hospitality, often holding parties that went on for days, with hundreds of guests. In 1886 he began the Birchwood Hunt, which still thrives today.

Dean took over the farm 12 years ago, as his father wanted to concentrate on horse racing, his lifelong passion. Dean still runs the farm as a sheep and beef farm with Romney ewes and Hereford cows.

An avid hunter, he has a hunting dog named Lucky, a friendly collie cross packed with iron-hard muscle who is passionate about his job. In 2021 when they were out pig hunting, Lucky went missing. Dean searched a wide area, constantly calling, but there was no response. After three hours Dean reluctantly gave up the search. He had driven about 8 kilometres back along the track towards home when he stopped at a random spot to listen in case Lucky was close by. Away in the distance he heard barking. Dean and his second dog, Claude, made their way towards the sound and there was Lucky with a big angry boar bailed up. An exhausted, happy dog had done his job and he wasn't moving till the boss arrived.

Hearing this story, I imagined poor Lucky focused for three long hours on keeping this boar bailed up, thinking, 'Where the hell is he? Do I have to do all the work? I bet he's home reading a book!'

HUNZA — BOOT CAMP

—

MANY OF THE young people I worked with had never been out of Invercargill. On the streets they were tough, but I wondered how they would cope with being in the Fiordland forest, staying in a hut with no electricity, a long-drop toilet, and having to cook their own meals. I thought I'd find out.

I chose tough guys — a few skinheads, a punk, a young guy who at 13 was already on his way to becoming an established car thief, and 14-year-old Casey, who was quick with a knife and had a violent temper.

We drove from Invercargill to Manapōuri and dropped Hunza off at home with Lance, as dogs are not permitted in a national park. While there, we picked up some sleeping bags — Lance and I seemed to own a lot of camping gear. We had packed our food and everything else we needed for our two-night stay in the Hope Arm Hut, a slow three-hour walk through swamps and fern groves, all under amazing mature beech forest. At no stage was I worried about my safety; in fact all the boys were very protective of me as, over time, I had gained their trust.

I had checked to make sure they had no drugs or weapons

on them — I had asked them all to be clean to ensure they weren't carrying any weapons and they were. After crossing the Lower Waiau by boat we started along the well-marked track. It was quiet — there are very few birds around due to the high number of introduced predators. The contrast to the kids' home turf, the streets of Invercargill, even though it's only a small city, made an immediate impact. They were no longer the tough guys, in fact they hardly spoke, bunching up together for security.

We had only walked for about 25 minutes when one of them asked how much further it was, and would the track get any bigger? I explained that this was it for the next two and a half hours and they should try to enjoy the quiet, to smell the fresh air, away from car fumes, away from any tension. But there was tension — they were way out of their comfort zone. What would the forest offer? Was it a whole new threat? They couldn't understand that no one lived there, and that they were free to walk without being confronted by police.

One of the skinheads — lean, straight-limbed and extremely strong for his small build, basically a hit guy — was on alert, his whole body taut, ready to jump. After crossing a small marsh I sat down on a log and told them to join me. I handed out apples and told them to drink from the nearby creek if they were thirsty.

'I'm not drinking that muck,' one of the boys muttered.

'Is there a McDonald's where we're going?' asked another.

I showed them how to cup their hands and drink the fresh

cool water, telling them we were not going any further until they had all tried it. One by one, they timidly knelt down beside the stream and caught water in their firmly cupped hands. I watched each one carefully, as they gained confidence in their new skill. Then I listened as they started to talk to one another and even to laugh, something I had hardly ever seen any of them do. I chatted on about the forest, the deer, possums, birds and how the forest was the lifeblood of our planet. They listened.

After another three hours' slow walk we arrived at the hut, situated in the forest just off the beach. I introduced them to the long-drop toilet, which a couple of them were well used to. I allocated bunks and then we collected wood for the fire. They followed me closely, slowly gaining confidence to walk away from me to scout out larger pieces of wood, coming back full of pride.

I had made sandwiches for lunch so we sat on the beach in the sun. 'You could take your Doc Martens off and walk in bare feet,' I suggested to one of them. I was already in bare feet, feeling the warmth of the river stones connecting me with the earth. They all took off their footwear, displaying a row of pale feet with soft soles.

I talked about Richard Bach's book *Jonathan Livingston Seagull*. I had read bits of it to them before we left Invercargill.

'Remember how Jonathan overcame his fear?' I asked. 'He felt alive, trembled with delight and proud that his fear was under control. I realise this is all new to you but you too can learn to fly, not in the sky but here. Right here! You are the one who places limits on yourself, no one else. Go and explore, but stay within sight of the lake. You can go as far as you want, because I trust you to come back.'

They looked at me but no one moved.

'Nothing will hurt you out here, just stay on the lake edge. I know you all can survive on the streets, so I am confident you will learn to survive out here.'

The three skinheads were the first to leave our campsite, carefully walking in bare feet on the stones and rocks, and even getting their feet wet. I heard laughter and watched as all of them slowly worked up enough confidence to walk through a small river.

I had been hoping we would have the hut to ourselves but it was not to be. A local teenager who I knew well turned up, dressed in his bush clothes and tramping boots, with a backpack on his back and a knife strapped around his waist. He threw his gear on one of the bunks and then came down to where I was sitting on the beach.

'What are you doing here, Ruth? Who do all the sleeping bags belong to?' I just told him there was a group of us out camping for two nights, but didn't give anything away. He returned to the hut and lit the small woodburner, which was the heater for the hut.

The boys all came back and I could see that already two of them were magically touched by the forest and nature. The word 'bushman' was spoken with reverence, there was no swearing, no raised voices, no overpowering signs of testosterone.

That night as we prepared our meal over the small wood stove, the visiting local lad decided to show off his bush skills by opening up a tin of beans with his large, serrated knife. He stabbed the can with an exaggerated thrust of the knife, looking at the boys to ensure they were watching him. And they were, but they were not as impressed as he had clearly hoped they would be.

Casey, who had successfully defended himself many times with a knife, went over, took the knife and burst out laughing. 'This isn't a real knife,' he said. 'It's crap. Come to Invercargill and I'll show you a real knife and how to use it!'

The local lad stood still, eyes very wide, and a flash of fear washed across his face. I felt slightly sorry for him as he packed up his gear and headed for the safety of the Back Valley Hut, an hour's tramp away.

After three days and two nights we tramped back to Manapōuri, walking easily now, heads high. The boys had learnt the basic skills of how to live in the bush. They were excited about going back to what they knew, but they had made it clear they wanted to learn more about the wilderness. It had been a win! I would read them the last pages of *Jonathan Livingston Seagull*, since they had stepped outside their city environment and experienced something very different.

'The hardest thing is to convince a bird it is free,' Jonathan told Fletcher. The hardest thing for me was to convince these boys that they, too, could be free: free of gangs, free of abuse, free to be who they wanted to be. They only needed to truly want it.

Hunza rejoined us in Manapōuri, glad to be back with the group. He listened to the chatter, and soaked up the boys' attention as he welded his way back into their lives.

Nelson

NELSON, THE PAGE & BLACKMORE BOOKSHOP DOG

When I walked into Page & Blackmore's bookshop in Trafalgar Street, Nelson, I was immediately in heaven. Books surrounded me. Piles of books, shelves stacked full of books, boxes of books on the floor, along with an array of beautiful cards, writing paper and bookmarks. If you are a book devotee, bookshops are your place of comfort, respite and — of course — grade 10 excitement.

Jo, the owner, came over to welcome me, as I had arranged to have a book signing in her shop. Although we both had Covid masks on, I could tell from the warmth in her eyes that we were going to be friends. Then Jo casually said, 'I'll go and get Nelson.'

A *dog*! Here I am writing a book about bookshop dogs, and Jo has a bookshop and a dog!

Out came a Hungarian Vizsla — I recognised the breed

straight away because I had met one before. He was sleek, regal, full of himself and offering me his soft toy bunny.

Nelson sat in front of me and looked up, his eyes full of expectation. Of course I couldn't resist, and responded with hugs and cuddles.

'Jo, this is incredible,' I said. 'I am writing a book about dogs who come to my bookshops. Nelson must be in it! He is a true bookshop dog.'

Jo smiled and nodded in agreement. We were definitely going to be friends.

Page & Blackmore began in 1998 when two nearby bookshops, one dating back to 1909, merged into one shop at the current location, 254 Trafalgar Street. Jo bought the shop in 2016, and although she has tweaked a few details, the shop remains committed to offering a wide range of new books, fiction and non-fiction, and gorgeous children's books.

She also has one of New Zealand's largest magazine selections, with an incredible 3000-plus titles. All this in a bookshop that is not that big. The shop has a narrow frontage, but inside it stretches back, inviting you to venture further down between the rows of books towards the magazines and children's books at the back. The walls are a beautiful shade of green — well, the little you can see of the walls, as there are books in every available space . . . just like my bookshops!

I only had a small number of books to sign, which gave

me lots of time to explore and find hidden treasures.

Nelson was three years old and began in the role of bookshop dog when he was just eight weeks. Having spent several weeks looking at the SPCA puppy listings, Jo had given up and started looking on Trade Me. And there they were, in nearby Ruby Bay: eight little Hungarian Vizsla puppies lined up in a row, peering over the back of a ute, their paws dangling as they all looked at the camera. Who could resist? Jo obviously couldn't.

She phoned the owner and two hours later she was meeting — and falling in love with — the three remaining unadopted puppies. She sat on the concrete driveway covered in puppies as they climbed over her, exploring and sniffing. Within minutes two of them had wandered off, looking for more adventure, but the third puppy curled up on her lap and went to sleep. As Jo was looking for a relaxed puppy to be her bookshop dog, this little man seemed an exact fit. Two days later she returned to collect eight-week-old Nelson.

The tiny golden bundle was an instant hit in the shop — so much so that one family of book-buyers contacted the owners and adopted the last puppy from Nelson's litter.

Today Nelson (the dog, not the town) has a huge following. He has regulars coming in each day to visit him and give him a pat; kids climb all over him and even snuggle up in his bed. Sitting quietly in the shop, Nelson, being a shorthaired dog, feels the cold, so Jo has bought him beautiful merino jackets. He has a warm bed, a woollen blanket, his own heater ... but wait! There is more! The overhead heat pump blasts heat down on him all day long. No wonder he curls up and sleeps most of the time, just waiting for the next customer to give him some love.

When I heard all this I felt a little guilty that Cove, my part-time bookshop dog, is not as spoilt. He has a warm bed beside our fireplace in the house but the shop is too small for him to have a bed in there. Cove came into our lives in 2015, a quiet, well-behaved black and white dog with a mix of at least three breeds, including boxer and pointer. Regan, his owner, who is a commercial crayfisherman on the Fiordland coast, is away at sea for up to 10 days at a time over the cray season, and we are Cove's minders in his absence.

Named after Deep Cove, at the head of Doubtful Sound, Cove made himself at home immediately when he first arrived at our place. In his gentle, enduring way he became our part-time dog, and when I opened the bookshops he adopted the mantle of bookshop dog immediately, just like Nelson.

Nelson often spends time in his *second* bed, in the office upstairs, or in the workspace at the back of the shop. If time allows, he and Jo go for a romp along the river, and about once a week they stop at the vet's to pick up a rawhide bone, which Nelson proudly carries back to the shop. Midweek, Jo has a couple of days off so they generally head over

Tākaka Hill to Golden Bay. Nelson loves the beach, loves digging huge holes, and no matter what the weather, he plunges in for a swim.

On the day I visited, Nelson was sporting a beautiful red merino coat and wandering around the bookshop with his bunny looking for friends. 'Oh! A new customer! Here I am!'

I left this wonderful shop loaded down with gifts for friends (books!) and books for me and Lance. I was extremely happy to find Bill Browder's new book *Freezing Order*, an incredible true story about money laundering, murders, and the ongoing saga of President Vladimir Putin's vendetta against the author and his family.

For lighter reading I bought *Dogs in Early New Zealand Photographs*, published by Te Papa Press with an introduction by Mike White and over 100 photographs. I finally extracted myself from Jo's shop without too much damage, spending just under $200. Pretty good going for me!

HUNZA AND THE MIDNIGHT BUST

—

TWO GANGS WERE well established in Invercargill — the Mongrel Mob and the skinheads. There were also a few punks, who weren't a cause for concern, but a new bike gang from up north was starting to appear on the Invercargill streets. They were scouting around schools to recruit prospects for the bottom rung of the ladder of the new gang. There were plenty of them — young boys looking for excitement and also a place where they felt they belonged.

I was driving along with a van full of high-school kids. All of them knew me well and trusted me. Sixteen-year-old Craig, who was sitting up front with me, was constantly fidgeting; he couldn't keep still.

'What's up?' I asked.

'Can't tell, but shit is going down and *I know about it!*'

'A big deal then, Craig?'

'Real big deal.'

I dropped the others off and asked Craig if he would like to walk Hunza with me.

'Cool, just us three?'

I nodded and headed out to the beach. I knew Craig well enough to know he would tell me what was going to happen; it would give him a sense of importance.

'I hear there's a new gang coming into town,' I said casually. 'That could be interesting.'

He looked at me and smiled. 'Did you know they were recruiting?'

I did know but told him I didn't.

'Some of my mates are going to rob a liquor store on Tuesday night, to start to work towards their patches.'

'I'm glad you're not involved,' I said. 'It will only lead to trouble.'

'You think they are stupid? They have a great plan.'

I stayed silent, and sure enough, he couldn't stop himself.

'Three of them are breaking into the Street Liquor store at 2.30 in the morning. No one will be around. They have a car and everything.'

I had heard enough. 'Best you keep this to yourself, Craig.'

He nodded, jumped out of the van and took off after Hunza, who was exploring the sand dunes.

A huge guy named Liam appointed himself to look after me soon after I started work as a youth worker. I could stand behind him and you couldn't see me. He was always there for me whenever I needed backup. He was a gang member, and as I had helped some of their members without involving the police or Social Welfare, he trusted me. I told him about the proposed robbery and that I wanted to stop it, as a way of stopping these kids prospecting to get into the gang. Liam wasn't keen on the new gang coming to town either, so he was more than willing to help. He came up with a plan.

At 2 a.m. we met up at the back of the liquor store — Liam, Hunza and me. He told me to follow his instructions, which was slightly concerning as I knew his gang had access to guns.

'I don't want anyone to be hurt,' I said firmly. 'Can you promise me that?'

'Stop worrying, Ruth. Just climb up here and lie down flat on the roof.'

I climbed up onto a big grey rubbish skip and from there he hauled me up onto the shop roof. He then called Hunza, waiting near the skip, who with no hesitation leapt onto the bin and then onto the roof beside me. His tail was wagging furiously, eyes on the alert and ears standing stiffly erect. We crawled to the edge of the roof, from where we could look across to the carpark. Then we lay there in silence, as flat as possible. Hunza, lying beside Liam, mimicked us, even flattening his ears.

It wasn't long before an old car pulled up and stopped under a tree. Three young boys climbed out. One was carrying a crowbar and the other two each carried something but I couldn't make out what. As they approached the front of the building Liam quickly stood up. He tapped the side of his leg and Hunza immediately stood up beside him. I lay still.

'What are you boys up to?' Liam yelled clearly into the night as he switched on a big torch, which lit up Hunza.

The boys looked up. 'Shit, a police dog!' one yelled. They turned and ran back to their car with the torchlight beaming straight onto them.

'Try anything like this again and I'll set the dog onto you,' Liam yelled. Hunza hadn't moved, hadn't even barked — but now he leapt up and down with great enthusiasm, knowing he was part of something very exciting.

The boys' car took off at a great rate.

The next day when I picked up a few of the kids there was constant talk about the police bust and the police dog who was apparently baring his teeth, growling so loudly that they were convinced he was about to leap down and attack them. Hunza was small for a German shepherd but by the time I heard the story he was at least twice the size, weighing in at about 50 kilos!

No one guessed that it was Hunza, the accommodating wee German shepherd that everyone loved. One of the boys in the back of the van was hugging Hunza and rubbing his head. 'You shoulda been there, Hunza!' I heard him say.

A young skinhead burst out laughing, 'Hunza! He would have just followed them and joined in the fun.'

I silently agreed.

The new gang quietly disappeared off the Invercargill streets after a couple of weeks and an uneasy peace was restored.

My Hunza had played his part well.

Reggie

CAVALIER KING REGGIE

Y ou could not be blamed for thinking that Reggie is a rather staid name for a Cavalier King Charles spaniel, but ask Jen what they call him at home and the answer is 'Lord Reginald Montgomery the Third'. A fitting name for such a handsome dog named after royalty.

Reggie was born on 21 December 2021, so is still a wee pup full of energy and seeking adventure.

Jen's introduction to the King Charles spaniels took place on a flight in Alaska in 2009, when she sat next to a man whose family bred them. He was on his way to go salmon fishing and he invited her to stay with his family (and the dogs). She accepted, and this was when she fell in love with the King Charles breed. When she decided to go on a three-week road trip, the family suggested she borrow two of the dogs, Charlie and Frodo, to keep her company. By the end of the trip Jen was convinced this was a breed of dog she would like to own. There was no hesitation over what kind of dog she would eventually get for her son Jacob.

Jen had looked after dogs in the past so she had a good understanding of what was involved in owning a puppy. She knew it was important to teach Jacob to be gentle and to help him learn to take pet ownership seriously. Owning a puppy, or any pet, teaches children about empathy, about being responsible, and to always remember that there is someone else to consider.

Jacob, aged five, has beautiful blond hair, blue eyes and a cheeky smile. He loves reading and writing, since both his mum and dad are avid readers. Jen believes that when reading a book to children you have the excuse to be silly. Why not use a witch's voice or talk like a pirate? It brings the book alive. What is a little different about bedtime stories in their home is that Jacob's father, Martin, reads to him in Czech, which Jacob understands and is already starting to speak.

When he's in the bookshop, Jacob has books all over the floor as he carefully searches for his favourites — dinosaur books, monster books, farming books, and anything by Roald Dahl. He is always in a hurry — so many books to choose from, so many pages to see.

Martin first came to New Zealand as a backpacker in 2001, putting his career on hold for a year. He had wanted to visit the most distant country from home and, as he loved nature and tramping, New Zealand looked like paradise to him. It was his first time travelling overseas and he took time to learn, discover and enjoy a different culture.

Keen to settle in New Zealand, he returned in 2004. Four years later he set up a travel agency to offer other Czech travellers an opportunity to explore New Zealand. He now shares his love of the country when guiding groups around the North and South Islands, his passion for the environment always to the fore.

It wasn't until he was in his mid-forties that he met Jen and became a father, realising a dream he had held for many years. He is a big, strong, gentle man who obviously loves being a father. He treasures books as they spark his imagination and curiosity, and are a never-ending learning resource.

Of course Reggie completes the family. When Jacob was in bed once with a tummy bug, Reggie stayed with him all day, just happy to lie alongside him. When the whole family went down with Covid-19, Reggie accepted his role in their recovery very seriously — he slept for hours and made no demands. Lord Reginald Montgomery the Third has become the perfect pet for not only Jacob, but also for Jen and Martin.

HUNZA — A VISIT TO
THE CEMETERY

—

AS A DETACHED youth worker I kept records of how many young people I was working with had been adopted, or were living with family members other than their birth parents.

As my own son Andrew had been adopted out at birth, I was drawn to this group of teenagers: I had so many questions. Were they keen to find their birth mothers? Did they ever wonder whether they had a blood brother or sister out there somewhere? Many were angry at their birth mothers, feeling a strong sense of rejection. Others yearned to find out why they had been 'given away'. They wondered whether their birth mother ever thought about them. What really surprised me was how many of these kids were adopted, and sadly this often played out as being one of the reasons they ended up in my van or in my office.

Vicky had been adopted by a middle-aged couple when she was just a few days old. She was their only child. When I met Vicky she was 15, with short-cropped dark hair, near-black eyes and just enough colour in her clear skin to show she had Māori blood. I had just spoken to her class at one of the local high schools and she came up and asked if she could talk to me. We arranged for her to come to my office the next afternoon. I quickly identified that here was a very articulate young girl, well organised and socially mature. This made me wonder why she wanted to see me. Maybe she was thinking ahead and wanted to talk about getting into social work? She certainly had the aptitude.

Vicky arrived on time, put her school satchel on the floor and sat stiffly on the chair beside my desk. Hunza went over to introduce himself, leaning up against her leg, looking up at her with his pleading eyes until she started to pat him. Small-talk filled in a few minutes, each of us feeling the other out. She carefully questioned me, waited for me to answer, then listened intently. This was clearly her way of ensuring she was placing her trust in the right person.

Then with a sigh she settled back in her chair, her shoulders relaxed, and she looked deep into my eyes. 'I'm adopted,' she said.

I waited for her to add to this statement but there was silence.

Eventually I broke the silence. 'What is it you want to tell me or ask me, Vicky?'

'Who am I?'

We spoke for an hour, pushing words through tears that fell like gossamer onto her cheeks. We hugged, held hands, and sat in silence, taking the time to place every precious statement in its right place so it would be remembered.

'Do your mum and dad know you're here?' I asked.

She nodded.

'Well, we have a good place to start, then. Let's talk to them.'

After she left, I thought about my own son, who was adopted out only weeks after he was born, without me ever being allowed to see him, let alone touch him. I had no idea where he was. Was he wanting to know about me as much as I wanted to know about him?

But this wasn't my story, it was Vicky's.

A few days later I was sitting in Vicky's family home with her mother, a small, gentle woman, casually dressed, in her early fifties. The love she had for Vicky painted every word she spoke with colour and emotion; her words were well chosen and spoken with tenderness.

'I knew this day would come, Ruth,' she told me. 'In many ways I am glad, but in other ways I am torn. I do know her mother's name,' she whispered. 'Is this the right time to tell her?'

I was surprised. 'Do you know anything else about her?' I asked.

She went to a drawer, removed an envelope and handed it to me. It was slightly creased, no stamp, with just three words written clearly: 'For the mother.'

I opened it carefully and took out the single page, unfolding it slowly as though the words might float off into the air if I disturbed them. It had been written just after Vicky's birth, by a very young mum who was unable to keep her baby. She wrote about the love she felt when she held her newborn, still wet after the birth, the tiny fingers that searched for hers, and the dusting of fine hair on her head. I gulped back my own tears as I recalled the same feelings when I held Joshua, my second son, not believing that he was truly *mine*. Only hours later he died.

I reread the letter. As my tears dropped onto the page, I felt the gentle touch of an arm around me, and the softness of a kiss on my cheek. We looked at each other; no words were needed.

'I knew Vicky would pick the right person to help us through this,' she murmured. 'I think I'll leave the letter with you. Ring me when you're ready to meet up again.'

One of my support team was an elderly Māori minister. I rang him, and within the hour was knocking on his front door. I told him about Vicky and her mum and we read the letter together:

> *I was lucky to be loved by a man who understood my illness, and my need to have a child, knowing that I would never be able to keep it. I am giving you a precious child. When the time is right, please give her this letter.*

It was signed with her full name.

'Leave this with me,' he said. 'I'll be in touch.'

A few days later he rang and asked me to meet him at the cemetery. He had found her gravestone: she had died only days after Vicky's birth, aged 22. She knew that by giving birth there was the possibility she would be giving her own life for her child's. I stood and looked at the small stone. Here was Vicky's answer. I grabbed the minister's hand, drawing strength from him.

I told Vicki's mother and father first. They both wept quietly, with dignity and clearly with love. When Vicky came home from school, the story of her birth mother filled the room, not only with sadness but also with an incredible web of love. After gathering our thoughts we all piled into my van and went to the cemetery. I parked close to the young mother's grave and pointed it out to Vicky.

'I want to go alone,' Vicky said. 'I'll take Hunza with me.'

She slipped out of the van, with Hunza following. We watched as they walked down the grass path between the graves, a young girl holding her head high, with steadfast Hunza at her side. When they reached the grave she sank to the ground, reached forward and touched the stone. Hunza lay down beside her, head on his paws.

When she came back to the van Hunza wasn't with her. She asked if we would like to go back with her to see her birth mother's grave and place the small bunch of flowers that her mother had gathered from her garden.

'Hunza is watching over the grave,' she said with a small smile. 'Let's go and join him.'

Tui

TŪĪ THE READING DOG

I t was another busy day in the bookshop, near the end of my season. I'd be shutting up shop for winter in three weeks. A vehicle pulled up and an attractive young blonde woman got out.

As she was browsing through the books, her partner stood on the footpath with their massive, incredibly beautiful dog. This was a dog you could not ignore, not only because of her imposing stature, but also her happy disposition. Everything about her was *BIG*! Even her black nose. Her name was Tūī and she apparently weighed in at 50 kg, with huge snowshoe paws, a broad chest and knowing eyes.

Bernese mountain dogs are known to be gentle. Originally bred for the Swiss Alps, their big paws help them get around on snow. Their life-span is only six to eight years.

As Tūī wandered off down the grass verge I thought back to a few years earlier when I came across a black bear sitting quietly near a stream in Alaska. Tūī looked just like that bear.

'What brings you to my bookshop?' I asked the woman, who introduced herself as Helen. She told me that a week prior, when she had had an hour and a half to kill at Christchurch Airport, she had gone to browse the books and *The Bookseller at the End of the World* had leapt out at her. When she read the blurb she realised it was about a part of the country she was scheduled to visit the following weekend for a Bernese Mountain Dog Club get-together, so she bought it.

She started reading it on the drive to Te Anau and soon became engrossed. They decided to have lunch in Manapōuri and stop by the bookshop to see if she could get her book signed. Eliot, her partner, thought it was very geeky of her, and the other members of the dog club apparently thought it was pretty funny that she was coming to stalk me! I was delighted, because I now had the opportunity to meet Tūī, and include her in this book. After getting Helen's permission I immediately rang Graham Dainty.

'Want to photograph a black bear?'

'Why not?' he replied.

Helen became obsessed with the Bernese mountain dog breed when she was working in Switzerland as a teacher.

Strangely, she never actually saw one in Berne, although they were scattered throughout other Swiss towns.

While Helen was teaching, Eliot kept house in an alpine village near Montreux, a town on the shores of Lake Geneva. They were there for two years and Helen would have stayed longer, but Eliot wanted to return to New Zealand.

Back home, Helen wanted her own Bernese mountain dog and started searching breeders' websites and Facebook pages. She soon discovered there was a two-year waiting list. Breeders have established a tight-knit community and there is a rigorous vetting process for prospective owners. A degree of persistence and effort is definitely required. The 'application process' for Helen meant applying in writing, talking over the phone, and visiting the breeder in person. She flew to Christchurch for that purpose.

The breeder chose a puppy she felt would work well for Helen and Eliot with their active lifestyle of running, hiking, snowboarding and enjoying the snowy mountains of Queenstown. Tūī was eight weeks old when she came to live with them. It had been Helen driving the process, but Eliot quickly fell in love with the new puppy and she is now a real Daddy's girl.

Helen had to agree not to breed from Tūī, even though she had perfect black and white markings, with patches of brown in all the right places. The white markings fold over her nose, with brown splashes either side, and she has wonderfully expressive small brown eyebrows. Her ears have crimped hair that looks more like fur, and her coat is thick, soft and shining.

Helen named her Tūī after the bird, which she is obsessed with. She also loves a New Zealand film called *Home for Christmas*, in which one of the lead characters is a woman named Tui. She liked the idea of it being a warrior name, and would have chosen it to name a daughter if she had one. Tūī has the kennel name Montreux My Sweet Lady, and the full name Helen has given her is Ladytūīdeschavonnes. She has her own Instagram account and Facebook page.

Helen is English and met Eliot, a Kiwi, on a working holiday in Cyprus. When she moved to New Zealand, Helen became a primary school teacher, and at the time of writing she has been deputy principal at the Remarkables Primary School in Queenstown for nearly five years.

Once Tūī became part of her life, Helen desperately wanted to take her to school every day, so she hatched the idea of Tūī becoming a 'reading dog', who would sit with children while they read.

A Queenstown Lakes District Council bylaw stipulates that dogs are not allowed on school grounds unless they are there as therapy dogs. But in recognition of the benefits that dogs can bring to learners, a group called Outreach Therapy Pets started a programme in some schools and libraries called 'Reading to Dogs'. Tūī passed the test to prove she was calm enough to be around other dogs, and children, and Helen's school began holding weekly 'Reading to Dogs' sessions.

On her school days, Tūī also meets and greets students at the 'kiss 'n' drop zone' at the start of the day. Children who find it hard to say goodbye to Mum or Dad will often happily bounce into school if they can lead Tūī in there too. This was particularly helpful for some students returning to school after Covid lockdowns.

'Of course we're always really mindful that not everyone loves a large dog,' Helen says. 'But Tūī is nice and calm; she gives the children space.'

Students who find reading out loud challenging will read to Tūī, who just sits and listens, not judging how the story is read or picking up mistakes. This helps build the child's confidence. Tūī is so mellow she just lies down next to the student, although if she gets bored she tends to stretch right across the book. It all helps children see reading as fun.

Helen and Eliot have bought a campervan, which has more space than a tent when they go holidaying with Tūī. They like exploring the country, and regularly post their travel finds on Tūī's Instagram or on the Bernese Mountain Dog Club Facebook page.

'We refer to our trips as "Tūī's Tours". She loves hitting the road with us, and amuses passers-by as she sits gazing out the back window, or squashed between us on the bench seat up front. She loves the water and will race into freshwater lakes and streams in any season, but only pretends to swim by walking around with only her head out of the water. Anyone trying something as dangerous as actual swimming or paddleboarding gets a good telling-off from her!'

Helen and Tūī go away every October for a girls' road trip to celebrate Tūī's birthday — she's even received a TV One birthday shoutout from John Campbell.

Helen also told me about HUHA, a charitable trust she supports. HUHA (Helping You Help Animals) is a 'no-kill' animal shelter dedicated to teaching empathy and providing shelter for animals struggling to survive in today's disposable culture.

Helen's commitment to this charity is inspired by her exceptional devotion to one big, beautiful Bernese mountain dog called Ladytūīdeschavonnes.

HUNZA ATTENDS
NARCOTICS ANONYMOUS

—

THE YOUNG LAD slouched in the front seat of my van. He looked haggard and dirty, and smelt strongly of solvent — maybe glue, paint-stripper, spraypaint or an aerosol cleaning spray: so many ways to get the high. His jacket was covered in vomit, his speech was slurred and the whites of his eyes were red. It was hard for me to see him as a 16-year-old.

The abandoned house in one of the back streets was a regular hangout for many of the youth addicted to sniffing. As I knew most of them I would often drop in to chat, sitting on the dirty floor far enough away not to be knocked out by the smell. All I could do was support them, 'be there for them'. If the police shut the house down they would go somewhere else where I may not be able to find them.

It was not illegal in New Zealand to sniff solvents and it was very cheap and accessible. I sadly discovered children aged 12 sniffing. We felt we were making progress, encouraging their yearning to be cared for to overtake the need for sniffing.

Brett was slumped in a corner of the room, a plastic bag

deflated beside him. Hunza was with me, his ears flat, his tail low between his legs. He hated coming to this place but he knew it was part of his job.

I pulled Brett up and told the others I was taking him to the hospital and I would be back. Some of them looked concerned — I noted which ones, as they would be the few I could work with.

Brett had been referred to me by the police. When I spoke to his mother she told me that over the past two months there had been major changes in his personality — he was having mood swings and she could smell solvents on his breath. Already he had graduated to covering his head with the solvent bag, one of the most dangerous methods of inhalation.

Brett had admitted to me that he had a problem but there was not much I could do unless he actually asked for help. I had been in touch with Narcotics Anonymous and they were willing to support me if and when the time came.

When he was discharged from hospital Brett rang me and said he was going to try to go straight. He sounded positive, saying he had been clean for three days. After arranging a time to see him I rang his mother, telling her that this was only a start, not to get her hopes up, and definitely not to ask him too many questions, to let him set the pace.

Brett and I talked for nearly two hours. He told me he hated himself and had been seriously thinking of suicide just before he ended up in hospital. He felt he had nowhere to go but down. I mentioned NA, not wanting to push anything on him and knowing it would be a very slow process to recovery.

A week later Brett waved me down in the van, and jumped in the back with Hunza.

'Thought about NA. I'll give it a try on one condition.'

'Only one?' I asked with a smile.

'I want Hunza to come with me. I don't want to go on my own.'

'I can arrange for you to meet one of the guys before the meeting if you want.'

'Nope, Hunza or I don't go.'

'I'll need to ring them to see if it is all right with them. Come and see me in the office in an hour.'

It was easily arranged, but initially it was only for one meeting. 'Let's see how it goes,' my contact said. 'Everyone who is at the meeting will have to be comfortable with Hunza being there.'

When I picked Brett up for the meeting he was quiet. He sat hugging Hunza in the back of the van; I could only just hear him. 'Big night, Hunza. Don't let me down, mate.' Then he asked a question, and I realised he was asking Hunza, not me. 'Do I look scared? I'm shit scared, so hang in.'

I dropped them off and told Brett I would be back to pick them up after the meeting. The 90 minutes went slowly, with me imagining everything from total chaos to instant complete recovery. I pulled up outside the meeting hall and waited. After a few minutes a group of people came out and stood around chatting. Finally Brett came out with Hunza. My window was wound down so I could hear Brett talking. He was smiling!

'Bringing Hunza back on Wednesday night, mate?' one of

the others asked.

'Have to ask Ruth, but Hunza loved it, so who knows.'

'He could be your sponsor.'

Brett laughed. As they climbed into the van I called out, 'Anyone want a lift?'

'Fuck, she doesn't only give him a bloody dog to take to meetings but she's going to drive us home!' Two of the guys climbed in and immediately started to talk about Hunza.

'Bloody great dog, really chilled. Are you going to let him come on Wednesday night?'

Of course Hunza went along on Wednesday night, and to two more meetings after that, until Brett confidently told me he no longer needed his sponsor to accompany him.

'Don't need another crutch,' he said.

We had definitely made progress.

Hunza the hero, once again.

tala

TALA THE
JILL RUSSELL

When Lewis first came to my bookshops I noticed a wee dog sitting in the front seat of his car, her damp black nose pushed up against the window, watching us intently.

'You can let your dog out of the car,' I said. 'She'll be fine running around.'

'Are you sure?' Lewis asked. 'She has a mind of her own ...'

He opened the car door and out jumped a white and soft tan Jack Russell terrier, full of energy and self-importance. This was Tala, nine years old but looking like a five-year-old. Lewis calls her a Jill Russell. He bought her from Hollybrook Kennels when she was just 12 weeks old.

Lewis is a tall, quiet gentleman in his late seventies. He's an avid reader of just about anything, especially big books such as Ken Follett's thriller *Never*, which is 816 pages long. He told me he may have read thousands of books in his lifetime.

Naming his dog was easy. Tala is the Native American word for wolf, and Lewis loves American animals. He had a sly half-smile on his face when he added that 13,000 years ago she would have indeed been a white wolf.

Lewis was born in Fairlie and worked on the family farm from the age of 14 until he married Pat. They adopted two girls, Lynley Maria and Terry-Belinda. When Lewis was 25 years old he worked for Mount Linton Station for a year, and when the owners bought another farm close by, they asked Lewis to manage it for them. He worked there for 26 years, loving every minute, before leaving for health reasons.

He has had dogs all of his life, all of them exceptionally well trained and well behaved — until Tala! When his previous Jill Russell, Missy, died of cancer at the age of 13, Lewis had been so upset he vowed never to have a dog again. His friends gradually talked him into getting another companion, so along came Tala.

Lewis is convinced he would not have survived the last nine years without her, after losing his wife Pat to cancer. When Pat was sick, Tala spent hours with her, sleeping beside her on the bed. Pat died five months before her and Lewis's fifthieth wedding anniversary.

Lewis and Tala eat together, walk together, watch TV together and sleep together. Lewis is a diabetic and Tala knows when his blood sugar is low — on a few occasions she has tapped him on the shoulder to wake him up to get something to eat or do a blood test.

Tala now knows every inch of my bookshops and surrounding gardens. On arrival she carries out a quick inspection, and when she is satisfied everything is in order she sits down beside Lewis as he leafs through a book, both content and in a world of their own.

Jack

JACK JOINS
THE FAMILY

J ack, quarter heading dog, quarter German shorthaired
  pointer and half Border collie — is chocolate brown,
with pure white patches dotted with soft brown freckles.
He has gorgeous liquid eyes, is full of energy and is only
six months old.

When I arrive at his place, just around the corner from
my bookshops, he is outside playing in the snow. It started
to snow yesterday, big heavy flakes that settled for a short
time before melting away.

Oh hooray, he is allowed inside! Jack comes racing into
the kitchen full of happiness, skating sideways on the lino
floor as he runs into the lounge to join us.

Hélène, who is French, has studied and taught French
in Japan, has a Master's degree in linguistics, and came to
teach in Auckland through a work exchange programme.
On a trip to Fiordland to cruise Doubtful Sound she met
Andrew, who lives and works in Milford Sound. He invited
her to visit and Hélène accepted. She absolutely loved the

place. So much so that she surprised not only Andrew but herself when she accepted a job in Milford, working for the same company. Hélène and Andrew were just friends and workmates for the first couple of years.

Andrew loves messing around on boats so he worked as a deckhand to gain enough hours to sit his Skipper Restricted Limits ticket. He worked on the fast ferries in Auckland before joining the company Pure Milford (originally Jucy) as a skipper.

When Andrew returned from a holiday in Canada, about two years after Hélène arrived, he was offered work in harbour control with Milford Sound Tourism. But soon after, torrential rain brought down massive slips that closed the Milford Road. Then Covid-19 hit and the country went into lockdown. Tourism came to an abrupt halt and the borders were closed.

Andrew, being very proactive, was up for anything so when the company offered him the position of team leader he accepted it. Meanwhile Hélène had been back to France to see her family, and when she returned to Milford Sound here was Andrew, cute enough, she realised, to be much more than a friend. Their relationship quickly blossomed.

They were both working and living full time in Milford, sharing a small unit of only 8 x 8 metres. What they desperately needed was a home base away from Milford for their days off. They had visited Manapōuri and decided this was where they wanted to live. And so now, three years later, here they are with Jack, a sleek black and white cat named Louie, and now a new baby boy, Ernie.

A baby, a puppy *and* a cat? Hélène grew up with pets and thinks it is important for children to grow up with animals. When it came to choosing a dog they weren't looking for a specific breed, but a neighbour told them about her litter of unplanned puppies. 'They are from good parents and look gorgeous,' she said, and of course they carried a small male pup home.

These days, unsurprisingly, they don't have a lot of time to read. If he can, Andrew generally reads thrillers, but he also comes into the bookshop to buy books on New Zealand history, especially on Fiordland. At present Hélène is reading baby books, but she has already arranged to have children's books sent out from France, as she wants Ernie to be bilingual.

Jack is curled up on his blanket close to the fire.

'How did he get his name?' I ask Andrew.

'Well, we thought of lots of names and settled on Tofu for a few days, but when I was taking him for a walk it was pretty embarrassing to call out "Here Tofu!" So we decided it had to be a single-syllable name. When we said "Jack" out loud he sat up and looked at us — it was as though he wanted that name. So it has stuck.'

Fast asleep in front of the fire you wouldn't think this was the puppy who recently ate two weeks' worth of iron tablets and had to go to the vet to have his stomach pumped ...

I get up to leave and Jack instantly opens his eyes. Immediately he leaps up and within seconds he is in top gear — no first or second gear for this puppy.

Yes, I can see him eating a pile of iron tablets!

HUNZA — A BOY'S BEST FRIEND

MY DAYS OFF coincided with Lance's, so he would be returning home from sea as I was heading home for a break from the streets of Invercargill. Both of us were making for Manapōuri, from opposite directions. It made no difference to Hunza where he was, or what he was doing, as long as he was part of the action.

I had bought a second-hand Suzuki 50cc motorbike for Lance as a Christmas present, thinking it would be great for him to be able to ride down to the local hotel for his favourite meal of sausages and chips, which he frequently bought on his first night back home from the coast. I could tell my present was a total failure. Lance's last motorbike had been a 150cc Suzuki, when he was about 18, and before that he rode a 650cc Triumph Thunderbird. The 50cc Suzuki was obviously an embarrassment — definitely *not* the type of bike you would ride smoking a pipe and wearing a pink silk scarf, which is what he did on his Thunderbird.

But everything changed when Hunza decided he would like

to be a pillion passenger. Suddenly that little Suzuki motorbike came into its own.

We could do anything with Hunza — he had total trust in us — so getting him onto the bike was not difficult. He was more than ready to climb aboard. Lance stripped down to his jeans, we drew a 'Mother' tattoo and some other inane drawing on his arm, placed a funny hat on his head and then set about preparing Hunza for his first ride. He didn't flinch when we placed a set of dive googles upside down over his eyes. Nothing could dampen his enthusiasm and away they went on their first bike adventure. I could see Hunza leaning into the corner as they disappeared down Home Street — how he stayed balanced on the tiny seat was a mystery to me. When they returned, Hunza was smiling and Lance was laughing. My present wasn't such a failure after all.

Hunza continued to amaze and amuse us nearly every day. He loved a challenge, no matter how big or scary. We wheeled him around the back yard in a wheelbarrow, he followed Lance's son Dane up a steep ladder to get to the top of a slide — in a somewhat less-than-elegant manner — and came whizzing down the slide, only to race across to sit on one end of the seesaw.

One evening we replaced his usual ball with an onion, which he diligently caught and returned to us. When he decided the game was finally over he lay down on the floor and started to eat the onion! We could tell he wasn't enjoying it — in fact his lips were nearly turned inside out and his eyes were squeezed closed, but he persevered until the whole onion was consumed.

If there was a game to be played, Hunza was there, often in everyone's way but on full alert and a great team player.

Dane came over from Melbourne to stay with us during school holidays, leaving his dog Jedda behind and walking straight back into his close relationship with Hunza. It was always a special time for all of us, especially Hunza, who quickly identified Dane as his playmate and someone he needed to protect.

As well as being skipper on the Department of Conservation's vessel *Renown*, Lance was a qualified diver. It was his responsibility to dive and check on the numbers of baby crayfish (puerulus) scattered throughout the fiords. While doing this work he became passionate about the underwater world of Fiordland and became a staunch advocate for its protection.

At 12 years old Dane decided that he wanted to follow in his dad's footsteps and become a diver. After much discussion Lance came up with a plan. Hunza and I joined Lance and Dane down on the lake's edge to witness this exciting event — Dane's first dive. Lance placed a scuba tank on his son's back, fastened a weight belt around his waist (the correct weight having been established), secured his face mask and then tied a 5-metre rope to the dive tank. The other end of the rope was tied to a large piece of polystyrene, about 100 cm x 50 cm in size, to prevent Dane from diving any deeper than 5 metres.

Dane was already a good, confident swimmer so it wasn't long before all we could see from the shoreline was the white float bobbing along slowly on the surface. Lance and I were relaxed but it was all too much for Hunza. He leapt into the water and swam out to the float, following the air bubbles, all the time yapping and whining. We tried to call him back but he was intent on finding Dane. Hunza's head would disappear beneath the water for a few seconds and then he would resurface, front paws thrashing the water like a paddle steamer as he frantically swam around in circles, half barking, half howling.

Poor Hunza. No matter how loud we called, he kept swimming above Dane until the tank was low on air and they both came ashore, exhausted. Dane was happy; Hunza was no doubt relieved.

Hunza was always the same when he saw children out in the lake — he had to save them. Pounding straight into the water, he would swim out just beyond the child and then try to shepherd them back towards the shore and safety. Job done, off he raced to 'save' another child. He even grabbed hold of a lilo once and pulled it back to the beach, the boy on top of it trying desperately to push him away.

Trips to the beach over the summer holidays were eventually cancelled as we, like Hunza, found it all much too stressful.

Hunza and Dane would disappear for hours, playing in the forest, entertaining themselves at the playground on the seesaw and slide, throwing sticks into the lake and digging holes. Dane had a dog to love no matter where he was.

In Melbourne his faithful companion was Jedda, a Border

collie crossed with a German shepherd. She had beautiful long, coffee-coloured hair with touches of chocolate and a black nose. Her ears lay flat against her head. Like most Border collies she was highly intelligent and well behaved. Jedda would walk most of the way to school with Dane from when he was 12 years old, and then turn around and walk home by herself. They would hang out at a creek near Moonee Ponds in Essenden, the same creek where Steve Irwin the crocodile hunter and zookeeper played as a boy.

When Dane was 16, Jedda was run over on a main highway as she was trying to follow Dane to the shops. He was sure he had left her at home and didn't realise she was behind him until he heard a car brake, and then a yelp. The car didn't stop. Jedda was lying in the middle of a busy highway with cars driving past her on both sides. She managed to get herself back across the road and limp home. Dane ran home behind her and found her hiding under the house. He rushed her to the vet. Jedda had severe internal bleeding and a damaged front leg but, incredibly, she recovered.

Jedda was seven when Dane left school and started working in kitchens, often from dawn to dark, with a short break in the afternoon. He was no longer her constant playmate. When Dane left to go overseas a few years later, Jedda became depressed, losing weight and her interest in life. She was 13 when he returned and her sparkle returned — her lifelong friend had come home.

Three years later, at a ripe old age, Jedda passed away,

leaving Dane with lasting memories: his first dog, who taught him the meaning of loyalty, deep love and lasting friendship.

Sam

SAM AND GEM, 'RETIRED' SHEEPDOGS

C athedral Peaks Station, only a couple of kilometres from Manapōuri, climbs up from the highway, crosses a fast-flowing creek and continues to the top of Freestone Hill. The rolling land is covered in trees and is one of the most beautiful farms I have seen. The 800-hectare station is owned by Cam and Wendy McDonald, and is also home to Sam and Gem, their elderly 'retired' sheepdogs.

Cam has farming in his blood — he and his brother are fifth-generation farmers — but Wendy was a city girl. She was the youngest of three and her parents just assumed she would go to university like her older siblings. When Wendy announced she wanted to work on the land, they considered this to be a waste of her education.

'You'll never meet a nice man out there!' her mother told her.

Even her careers adviser suggested other avenues, but to Wendy they all sounded boring.

Although she lived in Auckland, Wendy had always

owned a horse, which they grazed on leased land. Every weekend she went riding, and her love of horses would set the course for the rest of her life. In her senior school years she placed an ad in the local newspaper seeking work on a farm over the Christmas holidays. She was employed by a dairy farmer, and, much to her parents' dismay, this stint convinced Wendy she really did want to be a farmer.

For the first couple of years after leaving school she gained work experience on several different farms, then to further her rural education she attended Flock House, which was an agricultural and farm training school in the small North Island town of Bulls.

She headed south at one point to walk the Heaphy Track, where a friend who knew of her love of horses suggested she visit his friend Cam, who lived on a large station in the Waimakariri Basin. Cam was setting up a horse trekking business.

When Wendy met Cam, she knew her mother had been wrong. Pretty soon she was arranging to move Kaban, her 16.3-hand skewbald (black, white and brown) gelding, down to Castle Hill Station in Canterbury so they could join Cam's trekking business. Using packhorses to carry food and gear, they ran one- to 10-day treks through many of the high-country stations, overnighting in shepherds' huts or camping out.

Cam and Wendy were a team right from the start, and eventually took work on a station in Central Otago.

They were soon able to lease a portion of the farm while applying for their own property through the government's land settlement scheme for balloting former Crown land. After two years they were successful in securing Freestone Hill Farm on the outskirts of Manapōuri. Cam was 31 and Wendy 26.

When they took over the farm in 1982 it consisted of 12 main paddocks and a few patchy shelterbelts. They each had a team of four dogs, and over time this was reduced to one team of four.

The next several years were hard work, including planting thousands of trees. They established a large, mainly native garden around the homestead, which they opened to the public. As chance would have it, an American couple from New York, Francis (Frank) and Anne Cabot, visited. Frank described himself as a 'horticultural enthusiast' — only later was it discovered he was chairman of the New York Botanical Garden from 1973-76. As part of the garden tour they were taken to the top of Freestone Hill and, gazing about him, Frank was speechless. He and Anne both fell in love with the farm and with Fiordland. The Cabots and the McDonalds ended up establishing a partnership and purchased three adjoining properties.

The amalgamated farms were renamed Cathedral Peaks Station after the beautiful high mountain range that stretches along the western side of Lake Manapōuri. Frank and Anne built their home near the top of Freestone Hill, a place to spend the American winter — our summer.

Frank became a frequent visitor to my first bookshop, 45 South and Below, which I operated in conjunction with our boat charter business, Fiordland Ecology Holidays. He was an avid reader and loved books. Between us we established the incredible small library in their house, filling the shelves with books on Fiordland, Southland, natural history and botany. He already had volumes by his favourite authors, New Zealand authors, many of the classics and a lot of music.

Frank was in fact an author in his own right: his book *The Greater Perfection: The Story of the Gardens at Les Quatre Vents* is described in *The Oxford Companion to the Garden* (2006) as 'one of the best books ever written about the making of a garden by its creator'. It received the Literature Award from the Council of Botanical and Horticultural Libraries in 2003. A beautiful documentary film, *The Gardener* (2017), about Frank's personal quest for perfection at Les Quatre Vents, his 20-acre English-style garden in La Malbaie in Quebec, Canada, recently screened in New Zealand.

Wendy and Cam continued to work the enlarged farm, also employing a farm manager, Andy, who had his own dogs. He asked Wendy if he could add her young heading dog, Clay, to his team, and Wendy agreed, provided he could find her a suitable replacement — a good-natured dog with enough basic skills to assist her during lambing.

A few weeks later Sam arrived, and he was exactly what she wanted.

As the years went by, Sam became older and slower, so Wendy acquired Gem, another elderly heading dog, to 'job-share' with Sam. They do a half-day's lambing each. They also help with stock movements, but nothing too strenuous. The big jobs are left to Andy and his team. For farm dogs, Sam and Gem are totally spoilt. They always accompany Cam or Wendy when they drive around the farm, making them feel as if they're still involved — still needed.

Now 11 years old, Sam still loves to work but has to be closely watched to stop him working to the point of exhaustion, which he would do. He spends most of his day on the back of Wendy's farm bike, then sprawls out on his own couch in the garage.

When Frank died in 2011, and Anne could no longer travel, Cam and Wendy bought the Cabots' share of the partnership. They transformed the Cabot homestead into the five-star Cabot Lodge, which is managed by Cam and Wendy's daughter Breidi and her husband Brad.

About 10 days after I finished writing this story about Gem and Sam, Wendy told me Gem had had to be put down. She had jumped off the back of the truck, landed badly and torn the ligaments in her front leg. The vet advised that the trauma of a long rehabilitation and continued discomfort would be too much for an old dog. They had little option but to have her put down.

Sam is now without his workmate and friend. He has moved inside the main house, and when I visited, he was snuggled up on his mat on the heated floor. I knelt down beside him and rubbed his head. I'm sure he was looking sad.

As many farmers cannot keep their huntaways and heading dogs when they get too old to work, a website has been set up to help rehome them. What a perfect end for hardworking dogs after years of solid farm work, to move to a home where they can curl up in front of the fire and have time to dream.

Retired Working Dogs NZ Charitable Trust:

https://retiredworkingdogs.org.nz/dogs-for-adoption/

HUNZA — THE GIRL WHO CLIMBED OUT THE WINDOW

—

MY WORK ANSWERPHONE light was flashing — six new messages. I ran through them to see if any were urgent and, after making a few notes, I returned the call from a woman named Hannah.

'Hi, this is Ruth, returning your call.'

Without hesitation Hannah launched into a detailed story about her 14-year-daughter who, for the past two weeks, had been climbing out her bedroom window nearly every night.

'Have you spoken to her about it?' I asked.

'No,' Hannah replied. 'She doesn't realise I know.'

This was odd. Why wouldn't a mother sit down with her daughter and talk about it? So many questions I wanted to ask. Where did she go? Did she have a boyfriend? What time did she come home?

'I think we need to meet. When would suit you?'

'Suzie plays hockey after school today, so 3.30 would be good, as she isn't home until five o'clock.'

She gave me the address and I said I would be there at 3.30.

It was an older-style home with a verandah and a tidy garden. Hannah was waiting for me, nervous but obviously relieved to have someone to talk to.

For half an hour she talked and I sat taking notes. As I wrote, alarm bells were ringing.

'Why have you let it go on for two weeks before talking to someone?' I eventually asked. 'Why not talk to her, or go to the school counsellor?'

She just shook her head, then in a quiet voice whispered, 'I'm scared what I will find out.'

She showed me Suzie's bedroom. The bed was right beside a large sash window — the type that's simple to pull up from the bottom. It would be an easy jump down onto the ground, about four paces to the driveway and then out onto the street. There were photos on her dresser but none of a likely boyfriend. The parents' bedroom was across the hall, two rooms down, and the room opposite Suzie's was her older brother's bedroom.

As I had already visited Suzie's school to introduce myself and Hunza to everyone, I was sure she knew about me, so I drove straight to the park where they were playing hockey. When they were packing up their gear after practice I walked over to the group of girls. Hunza, eager for action, raced ahead and immediately became the centre of attention. Some of them knew his name. It was as though I didn't exist — all eyes were on Hunza, and he was loving it.

'I used to play hockey when I was at school,' I said casually to one of the girls who wasn't completely engrossed in my dog.

'I played right wing.'

'I am a halfback. We're not that good but we do win a few games. We have good forwards and a great goalie.'

'I'm Ruth. Of course you already know Hunza. What's your name?'

'Angela.'

'I'd love to meet your team. Maybe Hunza and I could come and watch a game?'

'That would be great.' She turned and called out to the others. 'Want Hunza to come and watch us play hockey on Saturday?'

No mention of me — of course dogs love watching hockey!

There was great enthusiasm. I walked over to the group and asked their names. Suzie was near the back of the group, her hand on Hunza's head. She was slight, tall for her age, her straight dark hair tied back in a ponytail. You might have called her sullen but I think it was a window to deep sadness.

'Anyone want a ride home with me and Hunza?'

Four of the girls jumped into my van, Suzie among them. I deliberately dropped her off last. We started talking about hockey. Being tall and willowy, she played centre and was a good runner. Her face lit up when she told me about the goal she had shot the previous week.

As I pulled up outside her home I looked across at her. 'You know that you can talk to me about anything, don't you?'

'Yes, you sort out kids in trouble.'

'Not everyone is in trouble. Sometimes they just need

someone to talk to. Having a friend you can trust is always a good backstop, just like in hockey.'

She smiled timidly. 'Thanks. See you at the match on Saturday.'

'Three nights away,' I said casually. There was no response.

FRIDAY NIGHT HAD not been busy, maybe because the nights were getting colder. I was heading home and decided to detour past Suzie's house. There was a service station opposite, so I parked in the dark side where I had a view of their driveway. I didn't have to wait long before I saw Suzie come out onto the road. As she passed under the street light I noticed she wasn't carrying anything and she was fully dressed. I waited until she was further along the road, started the van and drove at normal speed until I was just opposite her. I wound down the window and called out to her. 'Suzie!'

She stopped, turned to look at the van and then walked over. 'What are you doing here?'

'Doing my rounds of the streets. Taking kids home, keeping a few out of trouble. What are you doing out on the street at this hour?'

'Just walking.'

'Jump in, it's warmer — and safer. Hunza's in the back.'

She slipped into the back of the van and sat with Hunza.

'Want to go anywhere special?' I asked.

'No.'

We drove in silence until we were in the city centre. I pulled over and parked outside my office.

'Want to come up and have a hot chocolate with me? I'm having one before I head home.'

We sat drinking our hot chocolate, Hunza sitting beside me, ears up and alert.

'Want to talk about why you were out on the street tonight? It is rather late.'

Nothing. After a few minutes' silence she looked at Hunza and patted her knee. He went straight over to her, tail wagging.

'Families are shit,' she finally said. 'Can't wait until I am old enough to leave.'

'You're only 14, you shouldn't be thinking of leaving home. Is it really that bad?'

Silence. Suzie slipped down onto the floor and hugged Hunza. He lay down beside her, content to have her full attention.

I washed the cups and sat back down. A more direct approach was called for.

'Can you tell me where you were going after eleven o'clock at night?' I asked.

'A friend's place just down the road. I nearly always sleep there.'

'Great that you have a friend so close, but why not sleep in your own bed?'

'Better to be at my friend's.'

'Do you feel safer there?'

Suzie looked up. She nodded, then quickly stood up. 'Can

you take me to my friend's place? I want to go now.'

'Is your friend expecting you?'

'Yes.'

'Does your mum know you go there to sleep?'

'Don't tell her.'

'Why is it a secret, Suzie? Why can't we sit down with your mum and talk about what is making you go out at night?' I deliberately didn't mention her father, as I was beginning to wonder about him.

We sat quietly for a few minutes, Hunza nearly asleep on the floor beside her.

'It's my friend's dad.'

I knelt down beside her on the floor and gathered her into my arms, resting my head on hers. She was crying. Hunza sat up and looked at us, his wise eyes taking in every movement.

It was not Suzie being molested — it was her friend.

'I have to go. He gets home just after midnight.'

As I was driving we talked. I gently tried to convince her to get her friend to come and see me.

Saturday, hockey day. Hunza and I arrived at the park in time to watch the game. He ran straight up to Suzie and leaned against her leg. Remember me? They lost the game by one goal. I dropped three of the girls off and then Suzie came to the beach with me to give Hunza a run.

While Hunza played in the waves I told Suzie her mum already knew about her jumping out of the window at night. She considered this for a minute. She said her friend was very hesitant to speak to anyone.

Suzie ran over to play in the waves with Hunza; both were soaking wet when they came back to the van. 'Okay, I'll tell Mum,' she said as she rubbed Hunza dry with a towel. 'And we'll go and see Lisa.'

'Great decision. Let's go and do it now,' I replied with relief.

Suzie's mum was also relieved, and after much crying and hugging she suggested that Lisa come and stay with them for a while. We headed to Lisa's place and I noticed Suzie was biting her nails. 'Go and get Lisa and tell her we're off to take Hunza for a run. Don't worry — we'll sort this out.'

The two girls ran down the driveway and climbed into the back of the van with Hunza. After walking in the park we sat together on a bench seat. 'Lisa, Suzie has told me why she goes to your place to sleep. How about you tell me your side of the story?'

'You won't tell Dad?' she asked, fearful.

'I really can't promise that. But let's start from the beginning and then work out what we are going to do.'

Lisa's mother had died just over a year earlier, and three months later her father had told her he would feel better if she slept with him. They could work through their grief together and really support each other, he said. Initially Lisa thought this was a great idea, as she was having trouble sleeping and was missing her mother enormously.

After a couple of weeks her father started to cuddle her, and that soon progressed to touching. She told him she no longer wanted to sleep with him and went back to her own bed. Then about a month ago he had started to come into her room when he got home from work around midnight. That's when the girls decided Suzie would sleep with her friend every night, to stop her father from coming into her room. They told him Suzie was having trouble at home and he seemed to accept this.

'This can't go on, Lisa,' I said. 'It's wrong, what your father is doing — you do understand that, don't you?'

'Yes, but he misses Mum so much — he needs me. And I don't want to hurt him.'

That afternoon we worked out a way forward. First, Lisa went to stay with Suzie.

When I went to speak to her father I took Hunza with me — at least he looked the part of a dog who would protect me. Lisa's father broke down when I explained what the girls had told me, and that Lisa would be moving out, initially staying with Suzie.

I then handed the problem of the father to my police mate. Hunza went with Lisa every time she went to visit her father, together with a social worker. Both of them received the support they required for the crucial time of healing after the loss of a loved one.

Bill

BILL THE
HUNTING DOG

I have known Dave for many years. When I had my previous bookshop he would often walk past with two beautiful red Vizslas by his side, both sleek and shiny, with an aristocratic stance and extremely well behaved.

Now, 13 years later, Dave comes and visits my Wee Bookshops with a different dog but still a Vizsla. Bill is nine years old, and goes wherever Dave goes, his muscles tensed and ready to run. He is a talented hunting dog, a devoted companion and extremely affectionate. Bill is always ready to start work, even if there is no work to be done, he is a dog of *action*.

Vizslas are hunters and pointer retriever dogs, working on birds, deer, pigs or possums. If anything moves, they are there. Bill points at a pig or deer, and it is then up to Dave to kill the animal. Often Vizslas are supported by a holding dog; the two work together.

Dave has always been a hunter. From the age of six he was hunting possums using caged traps, and gin traps (thankfully now illegal). He was too small to skin the possums, but by the age of nine he was allowed to use a .22 under the supervision of his father.

In 1972, when the family moved down to Southland to farm, people didn't worry too much about the letter of the law. If your parents considered you responsible enough to use a gun, then you were given one. Dave quickly learnt how to hunt small game, hares and rabbits, and when they went up to Canterbury on holiday he started hunting goats and wallabies.

His first dog was one of his father's Border collies, which was much like a pointer. Dave and Cap hunted happily together for several years; he also went with Dave to his first farming job.

He left school a few weeks before he turned 15. When the careers adviser asked what he was going to do Dave replied, 'I'm going to be a deer culler.' The careers adviser told him no one did that anymore, but Dave was determined. He now had a .303 and started hunting with a friend about the same age. Together they shot their first stag at the age of 16. After delivering it to the chiller in Mossburn that accepted feral deer, they were paid a princely $400. At the time Dave was earning around $100 a week working on farms.

In 1986, when the New Zealand Forest Service came under the umbrella of the Department of Conservation, it wound down its deer-culling operations, though it still contracted out ground shooting.

Dave expanded into part-time farm work, private feral deer shooting, shearing, and hunting whenever there was time. By then he owned a Vizsla named Jim. He had researched the Vizsla breed and always wanted one. Between them they were shooting an impressive number of deer, so Dave was offered a job culling deer in the Murchison Mountains in Fiordland National Park. This was where Geoffrey Orbell, a keen tramper, had in 1948 discovered a takahē, a native ground bird presumed extinct.

An area of 500 square kilometres had been set aside for the conservation of the takahē, which today number over 400. Dave was tasked with removing the deer from the area. First, he had to prove that his dog Jim was under full control and would not harm the birds.

In all, Dave was a contract hunter for 14 years, working on government and private contracts all over New Zealand.

Moose, another Vizsla, was Dave's last full-time deer dog, and became a legend throughout the hunting fraternity. If there was a deer anywhere in the vicinity, Moose would find it and point. Over his career, Moose found well over 1000 deer for Dave.

Dave hunted for a time with a North Island hunter named Bill, who was recognised as one of the best hunters in the country. He had a lot of respect for Bill, so when he got his last Vizsla he named him after his mate. Bill came from Blackstone Kennels in Central Otago, which is known for breeding exceptionally good dogs.

Bill has never worked full time as Dave is no longer deer culling, but he is trapping possums. Over the past seven years he and Bill have killed around 14,000 of the introduced pests.

Blaze, a Border collie, is Dave's second dog, he is still a pup. Already he has a good nose so Dave reckons he will be a very versatile dog — sheepdog and hunting dog. Blaze lives outside, whereas Bill, having worked for nine years, has earned the privilege of living inside.

According to Dave, basic training is the same for all breeds and it starts the day you take your pup home. So much more can be achieved when you have a strong bond between you and your dog. He is a member of your pack. You need to decide early on whether you are going to train the dog or the dog is going to train you. If you have full control, together with a deep friendship, you'll get the best out of your dog.

The three basic commands are always the same: sit, come and heel (or variations of these). You can then train the dog to respond to any of these commands using a whistle, voice or hand command. Hunting dogs need to recognise hand signals, as they may be working in windy conditions, or they may be a long way away and you don't want to make a noise. Many hunting dogs go deaf because of gunshots.

As training progresses you introduce different commands. You have to remember that at the start, your pup doesn't know anything — how to get in and out of a vehicle, how to be quiet, walk alongside or behind, how to stop; everything has to be learnt. Life is a lot safer for the pup once you have established a bond. They are eager to please you, so training becomes a lot easier. The commands enforce your position with your mate, and that sets you both up for life.

Well-trained hunting dogs are amazing. Whether you are running traps or laying poison, you work your line with your dog at heel. You don't need markers on trees or anywhere along the line; no one will even know you have been there. You can climb over hills, cross rivers, push through thick bush, and then make your way back to camp. You do a poison line once to lay the poison, and when you have to return to skin your catch, you just say to your dog 'Get on', and from there you just flow, skinning and following your dog as he tracks his own scent. Part of it is memory but it's also smell. You can do a trap line a year later and your dog will know exactly where to go.

Dave assures me he will never get lost when he has a dog with him, as the dog knows where they are all the time. If he and his Vizsla ever got separated he could leave his bush jacket on the ground and his dog would always come back to it. He would sit on it and wait and wait for Dave to return.

It is a partnership: total mutual trust and a deep friendship. By reading his dog's body language Dave can always tell where the game animal is, or which direction it is coming from. In the same way, the dog is reading Dave's body language and often can tell what is required of him even before Dave tells him.

I am in Dave's lounge for this chat about hunting dogs. Bill has been told to sit on the mat just along from where I am sitting. He knows that as long as the smallest edge of his bottom remains on the mat he can lean across to me for a cuddle without getting into trouble. I reach out and pat him and his brown eyes look up at me, full of intelligence. This amazing, sleek, well-trained dog knows his boundaries, except that now only his tail is in contact with the mat.

Dave hardly looks at him. 'Bill!' And with that, Bill slips back onto the mat.

LOCKDOWN DOG

Tūī quietly arrived at Charlotte and Ross's place on their thirtieth wedding anniversary. They were sitting on the deck drinking champagne when a middle-sized English springer spaniel just turned up. She sat on Ross's feet and looked quite at home. They knew her. Her name was Tūī and she lived just down the road.

Two days later, in August 2021, New Zealand went into lockdown because of the coronavirus. Laura, Tūī's owner, rang Charlie (Charlotte) and asked if she would like a lockdown dog. During the earlier lockdown, Tūī had kept jumping the fence and running away. She always came back, but Laura noticed a change in her personality. Laura had another dog — actually Tūī's mother — and she thought that maybe she wasn't giving the younger dog enough attention. She was concerned about what might happen during another lockdown. Ross and Charlie were keen to dog-sit, so Tūī moved in.

In fact Tūī settled in so well that what started as a temporary dog-sit turned into a permanent arrangement.

Initially Tūī was slightly confused, and ran 'home' a few times to Laura's. But eventually she seemed to decide that her home was now with Charlie and Ross. She unpacked her bags and settled down.

I met Charlie and Ross when they first arrived in Manapōuri in 2009. Being book lovers, they made their way to 45 South and Below bookshop. Since their first short visit to Fiordland a decade earlier they had both dreamed of living in the area, but couldn't see how they could.

Charlie worked as a farm technician with Landcorp in Wellington, and when she was offered a transfer to Te Anau the couple seized the opportunity. Both were ready for a lifestyle change. The farm where they were to be based was a few kilometres outside Manapōuri on the edge of the Fiordland National Park, a perfect spot for them. Ross picked up some casual work on the farm and eventually became a full-time farmhand. Charlie used to joke with their friends that Ross was the only shepherd in New Zealand who had never owned a dog.

Charlie was born in Sweden and grew up in Cambridge in England. Ross was born in Taumarunui. They met at a jam factory near Cambridge, where Charlie was employed in quality control. Ross, having just travelled through India and Nepal, had arrived in London to look for work. Deciding there were too many Kiwis there, he bought a bicycle and pedalled 100-odd kilometres to Cambridge. There, he found work at the jam factory.

Charlie spied the man from New Zealand and liked what she saw. When one day he said to her, 'Hello, Charlie', she was surprised, as it confirmed that he had noticed her as well. Their first date was an obstacle course fundraiser, after which Charlie invited him to a May Ball, which was definitely a new experience for the boy from Taumarunui. By 4 a.m. they had danced and sung their way to becoming a couple. They married in England two years later, and Ross brought Charlie to New Zealand, where they settled in Wellington.

When I opened my first Wee Bookshop in 2016 Charlie contacted me, saying she was downsizing as they were leaving the farm and moving to a house they had bought in Manapōuri. She had a whole lot of books needing a new home.

It was Charlie who introduced me to Charlie Mackesy's book *The Boy, the Mole, the Fox and the Horse*, which is now one of my favourite books. It is one of the few books I sell new in the Children's Bookshop, and every time I read it I nearly cry.

(An aside: There is a wonderful man from Invercargill who comes into the bookshop whenever he is working in the Fiordland area. He brings me rocks he has collected, and once a beautiful driftwood log. His daughter Molly has been seriously ill with cancer for many years, so I give him books for her to read, as she loves reading. He has a gentle personality, a quiet voice and always a smile. Last time he dropped in he gave me a copy of *The Boy, the Mole, the Fox and the Horse*, which I treasure.)

Charlie grew up in a home full of books. The library I was now going through for her was what she and Ross had collected since they were married. There were dozens of books I would have loved to have on my own shelves, but as I was supposed to be downsizing at home, they went into my shops.

Charlie is in her mid-fifties and Tūī is her first dog. I introduced her to Mike White's book *How to Walk a Dog*, which is a must-read for every dog owner. The book begins when Mike started walking his SPCA rescue huntaway, Cooper, in Wellington's dog parks. Years later, he belongs to a remarkable community of people and their dogs who meet up at the dog park and chat about this and that. Anyone who has ever owned or loved a dog will relate to his story.

Now Charlie has this beautiful dog in her life who seems just perfect for her. She and Tūī often bring her friends to the bookshop, and they all sit out on the grass verge, passing the time of day. Ross, Charlie and Tūī go for a walk every evening, looking happy and contented. There is no doubt where Tūī lives now.

I am sitting in Charlie's lounge making notes on my laptop. A wet, untidy Tūī is sprawled on the floor near her bed. She is half listening; I see a tiny movement of her tail and she glances up at me. Her black and white spotted legs are laid out straight in front of her, her four black feet with their black pads are touched with a soft brown. She gets up and comes over to me, cuddling in close and placing her head on my keyboard.

She looks up at me with her dark brown eyes. Is this all about me?

ANNE, SPELT WITH AN E

'Hello! Ruth, are you there? Hel-llloooo?'

I was in the Children's Bookshop, surrounded by piles of books that needed to be squeezed onto shelves. The call seemed to come from a long way away, not just outside. I went out to have a look and saw a few customers inside and outside the shops. None of them seemed to be looking for me.

I couldn't see anyone on the footpath so I walked out to the road. Standing on the other side of the street was an elderly woman leaning up against an e-bike.

'Oh you are there!' she said. 'Thank goodness!'

I didn't recognise her but walked towards her. 'Are you all right?'

'Oh yes, now that you are here. I have just come over from Te Anau on the bike trail to meet you and see your shop, but you have dogs everywhere.'

I looked back and saw that even though I had only four customers, there were three dogs racing around having a wonderful time together. Just as I was explaining that my bookshops are dog friendly, and there were only three of them, a fourth dog wandered out of the main shop, sauntered slowly over to the bucket of rainwater, had a long drink and then stretched out in the sun.

'Oh!' the woman exclaimed, a touch of shock in her voice. '*Four* dogs!'

I tried to explain that they were all friendly, and often came to the shop with their owners. 'I can introduce you if you want,' I offered.

'No! No, that won't be necessary. I'll just wait until they go.'

'Well, come inside and have a cup of tea or coffee while you're waiting,' I suggested. 'I'll walk with you and you will be fine.'

We walked slowly across the road towards the bookshops; she was pushing her bike and making sure the bike and I were between her and the dogs. As we approached the main shop a big black labrador lumbered over to get her usual doggy treat from me.

'Here comes Lady,' I said. 'She is very gentle and she just wants a treat. She comes here a lot. If she could read she would be here every day!'

The woman gave me a small smile but her eyes didn't move from Lady, who was now standing at my feet, looking up patiently while I found her a treat. 'She is just like you — a lady. Can I introduce you to her? What is your name?'

'She's not interested in my name. That's silly.'

'I'm sure Lady would love to meet you, and I can't just introduce you as the lady with the bike.'

After some hesitation I heard a small whisper: 'I am Anne, spelt with an e.' I really had to smile at this, but fair enough to make sure her name is correctly spelt.

I crouched down and gave Lady her treat, which she took very gently from my hand.

'Lady, I would like to introduce you to Anne, spelt with an e. Anne, this is Lady, spelt with a y.'

Lady looked up at Anne, then stood up and took a step towards her. Anne froze.

'It's all right, Anne, she just wants to sniff you and say hello.'

I took Anne's hand and together we placed our hands on Lady's broad head. 'Feel how soft she is,' I said, 'and look at her wonderful ears — they feel like velvet. She's looking at you, Anne, waiting for you to say hello.'

'Hello, Lady. I'm scared of dogs, so don't bite me, will you.'

Lady stayed still, leaning in towards us as we rubbed her neck. I could feel Anne's hand slowly releasing its strong grip on my hand.

'Hello, Lady,' she said again, with a stronger voice. 'My name is Anne, spelt with an e.'

In the end Anne stayed for over an hour browsing books. She explained that she had never had a pet and was always scared of dogs. The farm dogs her father had were strictly working dogs — not to be patted.

'I admired them from afar, too scared to approach them, let alone touch one. And now I have touched one! Incredible.'

I smiled as just then Regan turned up with Cove, the part-time bookshop dog who has always been under the impression that everyone who comes here does so specifically to pat and admire him. Cove came straight up to me and as I patted him I introduced him to Anne. 'This is Cove. He is 15 years old and he loves everyone.'

When Cove saw Anne he walked over and sat beside her, leaning up against her leg. She stared at me, her mouth open as though she wanted to say something but not a sound came out.

I just nodded. 'He's fine, Anne. He just wants you to pat him.' Her hand went very slowly down towards his head, and ever so softly she touched him.

'Hello, Cove, my name is Anne.'

I waited for her to say 'spelt with an e' but there was a hushed silence as she moved her hand gently over the dog's head.

ELLIE

ELLIE OF HOME CREEK RESERVE

About a kilometre east of Manapōuri township a signpost reads 'Home Creek'. A short way down a dirt road you enter a carpark, from where you access a unique stream meandering through a 14-hectare reserve. Few people know that this incredible walkway was mainly established by an American woman named Edith who came to live in Manapōuri.

Edith became the owner of a springer spaniel puppy so tiny that when she carried it into my 45 South and Below bookshop all I could see was its tiny head. Ellie was named after Eleanor Roosevelt, because she was feisty, had a mind of her own, and was lovable and loyal.

As Ellie grew, Edith wanted to find somewhere she could romp safely without the constraints of a lead. This was when she discovered the neglected Home Creek Reserve. She did some research and discovered it was owned by the Waiau Trust. Edith then approached the trust and asked for their permission to plant it out in natives. Trust members were delighted with the offer. They were not in a position to pay her, but could supply her with potting mix and do the work of forming a track. A massive restoration project was underway.

Over many years Edith collected local native seeds, and propagated and planted them out around the creek. She cleared weeds, established the walking track, and put in thousands of native plants, including tussocks, cabbage trees, flaxes and a variety of trees and shrubs. All at her own expense, and assisted once a year by a group of Forest and Bird members, Edith worked tirelessly.

When she was finished, the region now had a beautiful reserve, and Ellie had somewhere to run free. The 1.6-km loop track is now a favourite among dog owners. The reserve is open to the public and is one of the prettiest walks in the area.

Ellie spent most of her life romping around Home Creek, witnessing grass and weeds being transformed into trees and shrubs. Everyone in Manapōuri knew Ellie, who greeted everyone she passed on the street and welcomed strangers at our local shop so enthusiastically her whole body would wag. When Edith went home to Boston to see her family we looked after Ellie for nearly a month. We loved having her, even though she dug a massive hole in our back yard, a little deeper every day. We just ignored it, as she was obviously delighted to be digging. 'Maybe she is digging her way to Edith?' Lance commented one day. Then

Ellie took to ripping up newspapers in a major way. This was not a random exercise — it was a dedicated activity that required total concentration and commitment.

When Edith came back she brought with her ceramic bowls with Ellie's name on them, made by her nieces; just something else to add to Ellie's growing list of personal belongings, which now also included a car . . . Edith had replaced her old vehicle with one that was easier for Ellie to climb into, and easier for her to see out of the windows. I wondered what the car dealers of Invercargill had thought when Edith asked them to allow Ellie, her dog, to jump into their shiny new cars. But then this was a woman who restored a 14-hectare reserve with thousands of plants so her dog would have somewhere to run . . . you have to get your priorities right.

Ellie was 14 when she developed a cancerous stomach tumour that grew very quickly. After only two weeks the vet advised Edith to have her put down. The vet and nurse came from Te Anau to Home Creek to put Ellie to sleep in her favourite place.

Edith had a broken collarbone at the time, so Lance and I arrived with a wheelbarrow to take Ellie to the chosen gravesite on a hilltop. We dug the grave and quietly buried Edith's beloved Ellie. It was hard for the three of us to bid her farewell. Even now I miss her smile.

Michael, a close friend, made a sign that still stands, marking Ellie's resting place. Without Ellie and Edith, the perfect dog walk at Home Creek would not exist. Although not many visitors know about it, whenever I take Cove for a walk I glance across and remember the energetic, friendly spaniel who planted the first seed in her mum's imagination.

I t was strange seeing Edith without a dog. In many ways she looked as though she was missing an important item of clothing, and she looked so alone. So it was no surprise when she decided to get another dog — in fact another Ellie — this time a labradoodle. Ellie No. 2 was born in Nelson, and was ready to be brought home to Southland when New Zealand was into the third week of our first Covid lockdown. Edith required permission to arrange for Ellie to travel.

Her first call was to the police, who gave her another number to ring. She explained that she had been living alone during the lockdown, and for the sake of her mental health she needed company, and needed a pet to touch and hold. Ellie was duly transported to Dunedin, and a friend was authorised to pick her up and drive her to Balclutha. Edith was permitted to drive to Balclutha and bring Ellie home.

Because we were all under Covid restrictions, we didn't get to meet Ellie for another six weeks. She was clearly the perfect companion for Edith, who told us having a puppy got her through the isolation of lockdown.

Edith lives just around the corner from us, so we often visit each other. Two walls of her lounge are dedicated to bookshelves, and there are more books stacked on the floor, on tables and chairs and beside her bed. Edith is one person I find it hard to recommend a book to, as her response is nearly always, 'Oh, I've read that!'

When Edith drops into my bookshops, Ellie No. 2 sits in comfort in the boot of her new hybrid Toyota, her chocolate-brown eyes peering out the back window as she waits patiently for her mum, the amazing woman from Boston who created a beautiful place where dogs can run free.

HUNZA — A THIEF IN THE AFTERNOON

——

SUNDAY AFTERNOON AND I had time off. The washing was on the line, the flat and the van had been cleaned and I had time to lie on the couch and read. Hunza had been with me most of the day, obviously bored, but watching everything I did. It wasn't until I got up to make a coffee that I noticed Hunza was gone.

After searching the flat and the front yard I realised he must have gone walkabout, something he had done a few times. I went out onto the street and called him, slowly walking up the road, hoping I was going in the right direction.

'HUNZA! HUNZA!' I tried to keep my voice controlled, so I wouldn't sound too frantic or like a demented mother.

After only a few minutes he appeared, racing around the corner, tail high, trotting towards me with something in his mouth. Full of pride, he came up to me and dropped a frozen leg of lamb at my feet.

Oh God!

There was no way I could find out where he had stolen it

from. Images came into my mind of someone going out to fetch the Sunday roast from where it was thawing, and staring in disbelief at its absence. I couldn't let Hunza have it — that would be rewarding him for theft. And I obviously couldn't cook it as there were doggy bite marks and drool all over it. The only option was to bury it without Hunza seeing.

With Hunza locked in the flat I headed off in my van around 10 p.m. with a spade and the leg of lamb. I headed out to Ōreti Beach, turning off onto the dirt road that led down to Sandy Point. I dug a hole twice as big as I needed, so the leg of lamb dropped quickly down into the damp darkness. I covered the hole, jumped into the van and returned home.

Hunza, oblivious to what I had been up to, was curled up asleep on his bed, probably dreaming of roast lamb . . .

Anzac & Raven

'FOREVER TILL WE PART'

You may have met Dylan in *The Bookseller at the End of the World*. Dylan is a boy who reads poetry, collects old English china and studied coastal navigation with Lance.

He was only 11 when he first stepped into the Two Wee Bookshops, and I could see how excited he was when he saw the shelf labelled POETRY. In his own quiet way he selected a book, handling it with care, a young boy already immersed in the wonderful world of books.

He found a book he wanted, which was not a book for younger readers — I think it may have been Byron. I saw myself in him, a young child yearning to read books that actually meant something. Like me, he wanted to learn through the written word.

Dylan, aged 13, still comes to the bookshop with his mother frequently. Usually he has time to discuss books and authors, and maybe he will let me read something he has been writing. He often gets captivated by a title and will go into a bookshop knowing what he wants to find.

He loves medieval-themed books and he carefully looks through books with gilt-written titles.

He imagines himself into the situation the book characters have to face. Dylan also loves *The Hobbit* and Robin Hood. Like any boy, so many of the books he reads offer a way to escape into a world where anything is possible. 'I don't think I could live in a world without books,' he told me.

It was through the bookshop that I learnt about his family dogs, Raven and Anzac, who are very important to Dylan. Anzac was just three months old when he joined the family. It was Anzac Day and the name stuck.

Dylan was only 10 months old at the time. He and Anzac have grown up together, learnt about life together and shared many adventures. When Dylan was in kindergarten Anzac sometimes went on nature discovery excursions with his class, which was great fun for everyone, but over time Anzac became overprotective of the children and the decision was made that he had to stay home.

When Anzac was eight years old Dylan's father, whose name is also Dylan, decided Anzac needed a friend. 'How great would it be for the family to have two dogs?!' They saw a litter of nine German shepherd puppies for sale in Riverton, so the family piled into the car and drove for two hours to see them.

They chose a small, light-coloured female. She had a purple collar so Olivia, Dylan's sister, wanted to call her

Violet. Dylan senior thought calling a German shepherd Violet might be problematic, so they agreed on the name Raven. (Her middle name is Violet.) Anzac adored his new friend and became very protective of her. No one except family was allowed near her, not even their cats. Anzac had a new purpose in life.

Raven is now four years old and, in contrast to Anzac, is a timid, excitable and energetic dog. Like so many dogs she loves running and swimming. On a visit to the lake she will swim well out from the shore, to where she can't hear anyone calling her to come back. Once she is well out she just paddles around until she decides she's had enough. No amount of cajoling by the family will persuade her to stop before she is ready to.

When he cuddles Raven, Dylan holds conversations with her. 'Anzac has never "talked" like Raven,' he once told me.

Anzac, now aged 14, is starting to go quite grey. He has slowed down a lot, as he has arthritis in his hips and spine, for which he takes medication. Like an old man, he is now in retirement mode and sleeps a lot. Dylan doesn't like to think about Anzac having to be put down, as they have been together their entire lives.

'I can't think what it will be like without him,' he says.

'Raven will miss him as well,' I reply. 'Maybe you will have to get another dog.'

Catherine, Dylan's mother, smiles and holds Dylan's hand.

'It's all part of having a pet — we've talked about it as a family.' She shakes her head. 'It's too hard to think about.'

Dylan's dream is to be a published writer. I believe he will achieve this, as he has experienced the magical touch of books. He recognises the value they have in our lives and how words can carry our innermost thoughts out into the world.

I t is early July, and Lance and I are headed north on my first book tour, car loaded to the gunnels as we'll be away for a month. A team of friends — Vicky, Steve and Des — are looking after our family of four chickens and the 100-plus sparrows, dunnocks and finches that swarm in each morning looking for food.

Lance is driving and I am writing with my laptop on my knee (at least until I feel carsick). Before we left, I loaded my new emails. I open one from Dylan:

Dear Ruth

Lately we have taken Anzac to the vet as my mum has found an unusual lump on Anzac. They have given the option to remove the lump though we declined because we did not want to put Anzac through any pain. We speculate it's cancer but we are not sure. Just letting you know and I would like to show you a poem I wrote for Anzac. It's short but sweet. I hope you will like it.

Forever till we part

Time has slowed you down, my friend, your senses dulled and weary.

You protect me and those I love, this I thank you for, I'd take off my hat.

But you now began to fade, your coat a shade of grey,

I'm with you till the end, my friend, forever till we part.

I know we will one day meet again, perhaps soon, perhaps not for a long long year.

I'll know it's you, you'll know it's me for the love in my heart,

The love I hold for you forever till we part.

I'll make sure you will never be forgotten

I'll remember your looks, your bark, your cry, forever till we part.

I treasure you, hold you close and dear.

I love you so much, my friend, forever till we part.

Dylan

I cried as I read the heartfelt poem. Dylan, is with Anzac as they take their final walk together, a love story that will remain in his memory for his whole life.

Anzac was put down while we were away, on 20 July 2022.

Pippa

PIPPA'S TALE

I had always thought springer spaniels were brilliant swimmers, but not Pippa.

I did a Google search on the breed just to make sure I wasn't making an ill-informed assumption.

The English springer spaniel is a sweet-faced, lovable bird dog of great energy, stamina and brains. Definitely Pippa.

Built for long days in the field, English springer spaniels are tough, muscular hunters standing 19 to 20 inches at the shoulder and weighing between 40 and 50 pounds. The double coat comes in several colours and patterns, the ears are long and lush, and the kindly, trusting expression of their eyes is a cherished hallmark of the breed. Correct again.

Springers move with a smooth, ground-covering stride. Yes, that's Pippa.

They crave company and are miserable when neglected. Definitely.

Polite dogs, springers are good with kids and their fellow mammals. Yes again.

They love long walks, games of chase and fetch. Check.
Swimming is a favourite pastime. NO!

Pippa loves splashing around in the shallows, but no way will she venture out into deeper water. Something must have happened to this adorable spaniel when she was a pup and we often wonder what it was.

Alva has been a friend for 16 years. Back then, our company Fiordland Ecology Holidays was one of the leading eco-tourism businesses in New Zealand, and cruises on *Breaksea Girl* were fully booked for months in advance. Lance and I were flat out — bums up and heads down for 11 months of every year. I needed a housekeeper!

Alva came to mind. I walked around to her home and asked her if she was interested in a few hours' work a week, helping me with housework and also a bit of work in our office.

'I don't even do the housework here!' she said. 'I am back at work myself. Peter does it all — why don't you ask him?'

Her husband Peter, retired, was sitting at the table reading the paper. He was delighted to accept my offer and was able to start the next day.

Peter had gone 'into service' at the age of 15, working in London as a busboy at the Savoy Hotel. He cleaned shoes, ironed staff uniforms, organised guests' laundry and cleared tables in the dining room. He worked his way up through the ranks, becoming a wine waiter at the age of 18.

With this background I knew I had the perfect house-keeper. The next day, after parking his car, Peter opened the boot and took out a feather duster and a bundle of 'special' dusters. Very soon my home was sparkling, our clothes were beautifully ironed, the footpaths were swept, and I would come home to a vase full of flowers.

While I was busy in the office Peter was there too, sorting clean linen to go out onto the boat, or counting dirty linen for the laundry. He collected stores, lifted boxes, carried luggage, helped me with the passengers and made sure I had my regular coffee fix. The ultimate was when he turned up with a warm loaf of his homemade gluten-free bread and a jar of Alva's jam. When Lance was away at sea he would drive around to check on me to make sure I was all right. Peter was always there for me, and he was always smiling.

It was a huge shock a few years later when Peter died. Alva was shattered but, being a strong woman, she eventually braced her shoulders and got on with life. She had always been an amazing gardener but now she became an *incredible* gardener, growing vegetables for herself and many of her friends. She made marmalade, jams and relish that filled our cupboards, and often arrived with muffins or a delicious lemon polenta cake. That was when I discovered that Alva was a great reader, putting aside a few hours each day to enter a world in which she didn't think about Peter.

After a few years alone she announced she was going to get a dog. A friend had a young spaniel who wasn't working out as a great duck-shooting companion and needed a new home. 'I'll just try her out for a few weeks and see how it goes,' Alva told me. Within a couple of days Pippa had won Alva over with her kind, trusting eyes, her big smile and the 'love me' look she gave to everyone. They were a team.

Like all dogs who live in Manapōuri she loves the lake, but it became clear early on that Pippa was scared of waves and deep water. Paddling in the shallows was fun, but going deeper was something she didn't want to know about. I would often walk Cove with Alva and Pippa. Cove loved swimming, but Pippa would wait at the water's edge, watching him intently, poised to steal his stick when he reached the shore.

At one point Alva had damaged her back so I was picking up Pippa in the mornings to take her for a walk with Cove. Often we went down Supply Bay Road to the bike trail, a great place for a dog amble/run. Pippa would race ahead and disappear into the forest, pop back out to check that we were still wandering along, and then disappear again. Cove just trotted along beside me at his elderly pace. I would often hear Pippa yelping as she chased something — a deer came running out of the forest one day; another time it was a possum. Nothing was too big for her to chase.

One morning Cove and I were ambling along while Pippa was away yapping in the distance. Then her cries changed, alerting me that something was wrong. Cove and I headed into the thick undergrowth but Pippa had gone quiet. Cove walked in front and I followed, as he seemed to know where he was heading.

Then we heard a few small yelps and we started crashing through the bush, Cove well ahead of me. When I caught up with him he was licking Pippa's face. Thank God she wasn't badly hurt — but what was the trouble? She was half lying in a very awkward position, one of her back legs lifted off the ground. It wasn't until I knelt down beside her that I saw her tail twisted around a small sapling. She must have jumped through a narrow gap between two small trees and her tail whipped around a trunk and got caught.

She couldn't move — the long tassels of tail hair were a tight and tangled mess among the branches. I couldn't move her until I had released them all, as she was pulled up tight against the tree trunk. Her right back leg was being held up at an awkward angle by her trapped tail.

Cove sat beside her, occasionally licking her face, and soon Pippa had relaxed enough for me to slowly untwist her tail. It took me at least five minutes to release her, breaking off small branches and forcing the two saplings apart so I could lift Pippa through the gap to take her weight off her tail. Thankfully her tail wasn't broken but I am sure she was badly bruised.

Much later a friend told me that working spaniels often had their tails docked to prevent such injuries when working in the bush.

I returned Pippa to Alva, very thankful that my story had a happy ending. Pippa was already behaving as though nothing had happened. It was just another morning's run, with added excitement.

Alva is now one of my book critics. When I don't have enough time to read all the books piled up beside my bed, Alva can usually be persuaded to take another book home to review for me. 'I already have four books to read,' she says, usually followed by 'Oh! This one looks interesting...'

Alva's lemon polenta cake (my favourite)

175 g (6 oz) unsalted butter, softened
175 g (6 oz) golden caster sugar
125 g (4 oz) ground almonds
2 eggs, beaten
zest and juice of 1 lemon
75 g (3 oz) polenta flour
50 g (2 oz) gluten-free flour
½ teaspoon baking powder
2 tablespoons flaked almonds

Glaze
zest and juice of 1 lemon
50 g (2 oz) golden caster sugar

Preheat the oven to 180°C (350°F).

Grease a 20-cm (8-in) cake tin and line with baking paper.
Beat together the butter and caster sugar until pale and
creamy. Stir in the ground almonds, eggs, and the zest and
juice of the lemon.
Add the flours and baking powder, stir gently until just
combined, pour into the tin and sprinkle with the flaked
almonds.
Bake for 30 minutes or until a skewer inserted into the
middle comes out clean.
Meanwhile, make the glaze by heating the zest and juice
of the lemon with the caster sugar gently until the sugar is
dissolved. Pour over the cake while it is still warm.

Bertie

ZOOMING WITH BERTIE

Because Bertie lives in Tauranga, I organised a Zoom meeting with his owner Liz to get his story.

Liz is sitting in her kitchen with Bertie on her knee. He looks very comfortable, clearly having perfected the art of lap-sitting. He glances at me on the screen, his ears erect in a permanent look of surprise.

Liz came to my Wee Bookshops after she was given a copy of *The Bookseller at the End of the World* by her daughter for Mother's Day. The daughter belongs to a little online book group and they had recommended it.

Liz put it in their campervan and read it during their next trip to the South Island.

'I was so caught up in the story when you wrote about piloting the boat across Manapōuri,' she told me later, 'and I wanted to meet you.'

They had been to Manapōuri twice before.

'Once I knew we were going to Fiordland I said to Rob, "Let's go and stay in Manapōuri." It was the start of winter and I knew the shop would be closed but you had written in your book that if you heard the ship's bell ring you would come out and say hello. We were planning on going into Milford Sound but we had Bertie with us and dogs are not permitted in the national park. We stayed in the Manapōuri camping ground.'

She told Rob she wanted to go and have a look at the bookshops in Home Street, but when they got here he read the sign and said, 'It's closed,' stating the obvious.

Liz told him I had written in my book that I would come out if someone rang the bell.

'So I rang the bell and, true to your word, you came out to see us!'

After we introduced ourselves we talked about Bertie and their travels, and also about Cove, who was mooching about, wondering where all the customers were. Life for Cove is not the same when the bookshops are closed. Where is the action? Liz was excited about the possibility of coming back down to Manapōuri the following summer to visit the bookshops when they were open.

I decided to include Bertie in my book as a travelling bookshop dog, and now here we are chatting by Zoom!

'What breed is Bertie, and how did you get him?' I ask her now.

Liz smiles. 'Bertie is a four-year-old Australian terrier. He is the second terrier we have owned. Our first was Baxter, who was 13 years old when he died of cancer. We only lasted three weeks without a dog. When Bertie arrived he was small enough to fit in my hand.'

Liz confesses that in her grief after Baxter's death she was looking at dogs on Trade Me in the middle of the night, 'which I know you shouldn't do. I typed "terriers" in the search box and Oh! Up he came.'

A slight complication was that Liz and Rob were in the Arctic at the time, so they couldn't go and meet this puppy. 'But I really wanted him,' Liz said.

'I sent the owner a question asking if he had already been taken. The answer came back with a no. So I asked if there was anything wrong with him. No again. Then I asked what I had to do to secure him.'

'Send a deposit' was the reply. Then the woman added, 'You can come and see him if you like.'

That was tricky. Liz didn't want to tell her they were in the Arctic because that would have sounded very strange.

'I asked where she lived and she told me Amberley, just out of Christchurch. What a relief! My daughter lived close by, so I organised for her to go and have a look at him for us.'

They went ahead and bought Bertie, and when they returned home from their travels he was flown up to Tauranga.

'He was just gorgeous, and very, very cuddly,' says his devoted mother, recalling his arrival.

'Why Australian terriers?' I ask.

'Ages ago we had a labrador named Jasmine. We were

living in Swaziland, which was a recognised rabies area, so when we decided to immigrate to New Zealand we had to leave her behind.'

Jasmine would have faced a full 12 months' quarantine, some in England and some in New Zealand. After arriving in New Zealand they weren't going to get another dog but Rob wandered into a pet shop one day and came home to tell her there was an Australian terrier puppy there. 'I didn't know anything about them, so we researched it and discovered they have been a breed since 1920. Cattle and sheep drovers in Australia used them to deal to the rats in their camps, and they caught rabbits.'

I was curious about this breed myself so I searched the internet. I found that Australian terriers were the first native breed to receive recognition, and the smallest of the working terrier breeds. They are reportedly brave, hardy and determined, as well as loyal and adventurous.

Liz strokes Bertie as she tells me about the long tufts of hair on the tops of his ears. 'When I don't trim the tufts he looks like a girl, or a handbag dog, not like the serious wee dog he is.'

Bertie travels everywhere with Liz and Rob. 'He is a real people dog. As long as he is with us he loves going places — in the car, on the bike or in the campervan. He even knows the word "campervan". He gets to sleep on the squab between our beds, which is an upgrade from his bed in the garage.'

She tells me she puts him in the basket on her bike and I ask if she has ever been concerned he might jump out.

'He's got his little harness on, and a little red strap through the harness to secure him, so he can't fall off,' she says. 'He's very vocal when he's in the basket, giving an excited commentary as we cycle along.'

We talk about the fact that some dogs are vocal, while others communicate through their eyes, ears and tail. I tell her about Hunza, who talked all the time.

'When he was in the car he wouldn't keep quiet,' I say. 'It got to be unbearable so we ended up making his bed in the boot. I was worried he wouldn't be able to breathe, so Lance jumped in the boot and I drove around Manapōuri so he could carry out a safety check.'

'Hunza actually loved the boot of the car; he was always eager to leap in and settle down. Sometimes when we opened the boot for him to get out he just sat there, looked around and decided to stay in his safe place, especially if there was a cat in sight.'

Liz did once have an accident on her bike with Bertie in the basket.

'I was on a really steep track and as I went around a corner I braked, lost speed, lost my balance and we crashed. Bertie was okay. We tend to stay off roads and stick to bike trails, as then he is allowed out of the basket to run. He would run the whole way if we let him, but as we usually bike about 40 kilometres we let him run a good two or three kilometres at about 15 to 20 kilometres an hour.'

We talk a little about Baxter, their previous dog.

'The worst thing about having a pet is that it breaks your heart when they die,' I say. 'You know at some stage they will no longer be part of your life but when it happens it is devastating. When I have spoken to other dog owners that fear comes through very strongly.'

I tell her about the death of Hunza. We had to have him put down when he was quite young because suddenly he started urinating blood. That was maybe 28 years ago but even today when I see a German shepherd I immediately say to myself 'Hunza'.

'There is the commitment of total friendship and dedication with a dog,' I say, and Liz nods.

'How is it,' I say, 'that a dog can totally embed itself in every facet of your life? No matter what happens they will always forgive you. You are a friend forever.'

'Whereas cats are more independent and aloof,' says Liz. 'Bertie is with us all the time; he likes to have his little pack around him, me and Rob. Dogs have a pack mentality, but cats are often loners.'

'So you mentioned that you can't breed from Bertie?' I say, changing the subject.

'We would have liked to but it was a condition of owning him that we agree to have him neutered.'

'Are there many Australian terriers in New Zealand?'

'You see a few around, but not many. They have a very

distinctive, very bouncy upright walk, so you can always spot them a long way away. Most people around here have grey or white fluffy dogs, so Bertie is known as the rusty dog!'

It's time to wrap up our Zoom discussion.

'If you want to go into Milford Sound for the day when you come back to Fiordland,' I say, 'we'd be happy to look after Bertie for you.'

'Oh my goodness, that's a big offer,' Liz replies.

'We look after Cove when Regan is away fishing, sometimes for a couple of weeks. We love dogs; it works out perfectly. We recently looked after a wonderful black labrador named Gracie when her owners went into Milford for the day. Cove was here and he just ignored her. We're not considering getting another dog until Cove dies. He's 15 now, and he's starting to age quite quickly. He sleeps on the floor right beside my bed when he's with us.'

Liz laughs. 'Fascinating, isn't it, how dogs end up getting their own way? When you ask dog people why they can't sleep, or why they have to get up three times a night, they tell you their dog sleeps in their bedroom, sometimes even on their bed!'

'So will we see you in the summer when the bookshops are open?' I ask.

'I hope so. Bertie would love another campervan trip. He loves sitting up the front watching the road. We've tried putting him down on the floor or in the back, but he prefers to sit on my lap up in the front.' (Speaking of dogs getting their own way!)

'Just before we say goodbye,' I say, 'have you read Nick Trout's book *Dog Gone, Back Soon*? It is a must-read. A fascinating fact from the book is that a human can hear at 20 feet, while a dog can hear at 80 feet.'

Our time is up. Bertie is still on Liz's lap, wide awake. Not bored, just waiting patiently for some action.

HUNZA — A GIRL IN
A WOMAN'S BODY

—

WHEN I LOOK through the records I have kept from my years as a youth worker, some of it still brings tears to my eyes:

K.	(Māori)	15, broken home, adopted
R.		14, broken home, attempted suicide
M.		18, broken home, adopted, marijuana
P.	(Māori)	17, broken home, gang member
S.		14, solvent use, prospecting for gang
A.	(Māori)	18, broken home, gang member, solvent use

There are over 150 entries, all very similar. The youngest was only 12.

I had given my word to every one of them that I would not divulge information to the police unless someone's life was at risk, or if sexual, mental or physical abuse was occurring. It was a tightrope I was walking. If the police or any of the welfare agencies asked me for information, confidentiality was my major concern. If I talked, the young people wouldn't trust me anymore.

I picked up a dark-haired 12-year-old girl from the street. She was sitting on a low brick wall, head down, arms clenched tightly around her body. She was in jeans and a rough, well-worn jacket. I pulled over, let Hunza out of the back of the van and walked over to her. As I sat down beside her, Hunza pushed his nose up under her arms. I just watched, saying nothing. She soon opened her arms and started to pat him. 'Hi, Hunza.'

His tail started to move slowly, and as their eyes met she started to cry. She leaned down and held him, and Hunza just stood quietly, soaking up her despair.

'Let's get in the van off the street,' I whispered. 'You can sit in the back with Hunza.'

Without any hesitation she walked over to the van with Hunza, climbed in the back and settled down with him on the seat beside her.

My record reads:

> I wasn't going to keep detailed records on Katie but now I feel I must as I have been seeing her frequently. At last she is talking openly to me, not just Hunza. I have asked her if it is all right to keep notes as we will have to take what has occurred to court. She has always been in trouble with her mum since her uncle started to pay her for 'favours'. He touches her, has never tried to have intercourse but she is scared it will come to that. She has told her mother but she doesn't

believe her. For a 12-year-old she is well developed, so has lots of boys chasing her. She lets them touch her, finger her and often gets money in return. 'If it's all right for my uncle to do it then why not anyone else?'

My notes are detailed because I knew this time I would have to go to the police. Katie had just had her thirteenth birthday — a girl in a woman's body. I told her I would be speaking to my close friend in the police, who was the youth officer. She agreed, but reluctantly, as she didn't want to get her mother or uncle into trouble. This was a common response from young abused children: they were nearly always fearful that talking about the abuse would lead to the breakup of their family. As they got older they either became angry and often violent, or they went the other way, becoming withdrawn, insecure and often suicidal.

Thankfully Katie eventually agreed to speak to the police.

The case went to court and the uncle went to jail. Katie was put into foster care, into a home full of laughter and warmth.

I continued to see her but it was always Hunza she welcomed first.

'Hi, Hunza, what have you been up to?' They would sit side by side, content just to be together.

Sundays

SUNDAYS IN DANSEYS PASS

I hadn't seen Michael for a number of years — back when we both still had dark hair and only a few early wrinkles. As he stood on the doorstep, memories of our school days in Naseby and Ranfurly came flooding back. His smile was the same, he was still straight and tall, his eyes gentle. Although his hair was now grey, he was still the Michael I knew.

His sister Sharon had rung to tell me Michael was coming down to stay with her on the farm, a few kilometres out of Manapōuri. They had both read my book and he wanted to 'catch up'. Michael had driven down from Ōamaru with his three dogs and here he was on my doorstep. Michael comes into this book not because I met him through the bookshops but because he has read my book — and as a dear friend who has dogs. How could I not include him?

We both started school in Naseby in 1958, when we were 12 years old. Both families had just moved to the area.

Michael's parents had bought the Danseys Pass Hotel on the eastern side of the Kakanui Range, in an area known as the Kyeburn Diggings.

It was a small school with only two classrooms, warmed in the winter by an old woodburner in the centre of each room. I could walk to school, but Michael and Sharon and the other children who lived on Danseys Pass Road were picked up by the Naseby taxi at eight o'clock each morning. It was 16 kilometres of dirt road, often dangerous in the winter with ice and snow.

After only six months Michael and I left primary school to continue our studies at Ranfurly High School, which was 14 kilometres from Naseby in the opposite direction. We travelled by school bus, an old Bedford with a flat nose, usually driven by one of the teachers. Michael was a quiet, self-contained farm boy. I can't remember him ever having a girlfriend, though some of the girls were sweet on him.

When Michael's parents took over the hotel there was hardly any traffic on the road except for farmers from both sides of the pass. There was so little trade that Fred, his father, also worked for the council as a roadman, shovelling dirt and clearing ditches.

It was illegal Sunday drinking that kept many of the hotels open throughout the Maniototo at this time. Sunday was the day for socialising. My father and mother would get all dressed up after Sunday lunch, and with my sister Jill and me also in our Sunday best, would drive through to the Danseys Pass Hotel in Dad's small Ford butcher's van.

Many of the farmers brought their kids. While the adults sat in the pub chatting, singing and drinking, the kids would be having fun playing among the gold tailings. We would climb the steep 15-metre stacks of yellow dirt, race around the rocks, dig massive holes and generally have a great time. I loved Sundays.

Michael's father had set up a telephone line from the pub to the top of one of the hills, where it was attached to an old crank-handle telephone. It was Michael's job to keep watch on the road over the pass from the west, in case the police flying squad from Ōamaru decided to do a spot check for illegal Sunday trading. There was another telephone wire looped along the fence in the other direction to watch for the flying squad coming over the Pig Root from Dunedin. If they came to Danseys Pass they would continue on to the Naseby and Waipīata hotels, so the publicans would all ring the next hotel in the line to warn them. I don't know why the flying squad bothered.

Michael always wanted to be a farmer. I remember once when we were asked to write an essay on a specific subject, Miss Alexandra, our English teacher, told Michael to write about training a heading dog. He had his first team of dogs by the age of 10 and was the youngest competitor at the local dog trials.

He left school at the age of 17 and went with his team of five dogs to work at Glenshee for high-country farmer

Eden Hore for a couple of years. Hore's collection of haute couture fashion, begun in the 1970s, eventually won international attention. Back then, none of us thought Eden was really that interested in fashion; it was just a way of getting visitors, someone he could talk to, tucked away out in the middle of nowhere. The collection of over 260 stunning gowns is today considered to be the most comprehensive fashion collection of that era in New Zealand.

When Michael went mustering he always had a team of eight or nine dogs. He would often guide packhorses with a mule team over Mount Buster (1200 metres) a few days ahead of the musterers, to prepare the huts for their arrival. He could sometimes be paid for eight days' work a week, as when the musterers rode from one job to the next they were paid 'Day Coming' money. He would finish work one day and travel during the night to be ready for a big breakfast and an early start the next morning.

Michael married Robyn, a friend of his sister's, in 1970 and they headed up to the North Island, where he was employed as a stock manager for two years. Farming was very different in the north, where the land was more fertile, but Michael yearned to be back in Central Otago. When a farm came up for sale on the eastern side of the Danseys Pass on the slopes of the Kakanui Range they had just enough for the deposit.

Some time later Michael bought some of the hotel's land from his father. When the old rural hotels were built throughout Central Otago they had to provide paddocks for overnighting stock, stables for the horses and accommodation for the stockmen and drovers. As many musters passed over Danseys Pass, his father's hotel had 405 hectares (1000 acres) of adjoining land to graze travelling stock.

Having acquired a chunk of this land, Michael owned a farm on either side of Danseys Pass. Even though there was 19 kilometres between them, the combined acreage was economically viable.

By now Michael and Robyn had two children, Ryan and Rebecca, so life was extremely busy. Michael thought Ryan would follow in his footsteps as a farmer, but his passion was flying and at a young age he passed his commercial flying licence. He could fly on his own before he could take passengers in a car.

Then tragedy struck. In November 1997 the family were advised that Ryan, who was flying whitebait out of the Cascade River in the Mount Aspiring National Park, had not returned from delivering a load to West Melton. The search continued for weeks but Ryan was never found. The location of his plane remains a mystery to this day.

M ichael, now 76, parked his truck and got out, then went to check that his three dogs — Duke, the huntaway, and George and Jess, his heading dogs — were happy in the dog crate secured to the truck bed. He turned and walked towards me. He actually has four dogs, but Flynn was still at home recovering from a broken leg, which had so far cost Michael $4000.

He still has a small block of land that carries 120 sheep, so he can keep his hand in. He also helps friends who are still farming, who often appreciate the help of an experienced man and his dogs.

We reminisced for a few hours, as it had been a long time since we had seen each other. Then, before they headed back to Sharon's farm, I had arranged for Graham Dainty, the photographer, to join us as I wanted photos of Michael's dogs working.

Duke is five years old, and with the one soft word from Michael ('Speak') he raised his head and enthusiastically barked at the sky.

George and Jess stayed close to Michael as they watched the small flock of sheep. They were eager to get to work, full of attention, listening intently for Michael's command.

He hasn't lost his touch, and the love goes both ways.

Michael Moynihan, my old school friend, passed away after a brief illness on Thursday, 22 December, 2022. A sense of loss crept over me when I heard that this quiet, gentle man with smiling eyes and a kind face had died. I am so glad we had that special time together; you, your sister Sharon, and your wonderful dogs.

HUNZA — HOME GUARD

———

AFTER A VERY busy nine days Hunza and I were heading home, driving from Invercargill to Manapōuri in the van. I was arriving home a day before Lance was due out from the coast. We would then have five days together before heading back to our respective places of work.

Just after midnight I was woken up by loud male voices out on the street. I estimated that there were at least five guys out there, quite likely drunk as their speech was loud and slurred. Hunza was already on alert, waiting for me to get up. I threw on my dressing gown and went out onto the street, Hunza at my side, looking every inch the serious guard dog.

'Hi guys, what's up?'

'Need some water. We saw the hose but can't find the tap.'

I didn't ask why they needed the water but told them where the tap was. They all took note of Hunza standing beside me, and in return Hunza was obviously sizing them all up. I felt safe with him there, and proud that he was so intent on what all the guys were doing. They were drinking beer out of cans, talking loudly as one of them filled a container with water. I assumed it was for the radiator of their old car, which was parked across the road.

This shouldn't take long, I thought, and Hunza is there for me.

Then one of the guys threw an empty can across the road. Hunza leapt into action, raced across the road, picked up the can and brought it back to the guy who threw it, head held high and tail wagging. The lads all laughed while I cringed: in a heartbeat my 'guard dog' had been seduced into being their playmate.

'Great dog,' one of them said. 'Thanks for the water.'

They turned and left.

Gypsy

COLORADO GYPSY JOHNSON AND THE GIFT OF LOVE

S ara lives in Te Anau with her partner Harlan and their very pretty two-year-old dog Gypsy. Sara had heard about my bookshops from friends and, as she is not only a book lover but also an editor, they were on her bucket list.

A red Volkswagen Beetle pulled up outside the Wee Bookshops. Sara had a cheeky smile and an easy gait. She oozed energy. Within minutes we were deep in conversation about books — Sara was looking for a good read.

She studied English language and creative writing at school, then completed a Master's degree in theology at Cambridge University. Her main areas of interest are the philosophy and psychology of religion; the science, history and ethics behind the world's religions; and theological responses to the Jewish Holocaust.

After her Master's, Sara went on to obtain a diploma in creative writing, also from Cambridge. She loves studying and thrives in the academic setting, so she may not be finished with it! Sara's goal is to become a published author, and with her track record there is little doubt she will get there.

Taking a year off study to travel once she finished school, Sara first came to New Zealand in 2004 and stayed for three months. Back home in England, after finishing her degree she moved to London, where she qualified as an accountant. She dreamt of returning to New Zealand and did so in 2011, settling in Queenstown for the 2012 ski season. She found work as an accountant and applied for residency in 2014. Not long after, she met Harlan, who was driving buses up to the Queenstown ski fields in winter, and working as a kayak guide in Milford Sound in the summer. They were both touched by the majesty of Fiordland, so that was where they settled together.

I was admittedly a little overawed by this woman and her accomplishments: where did I start to recommend a book to her? Did I have a title in stock that she would take home and treasure? Then it came to me. Of course! *The Hare with Amber Eyes: A Hidden Inheritance*, a memoir by Edmund de Waal. Not only is it a history lesson about assimilation, anti-Semitism, dispersion and exile, but it is a beautiful and captivating story. It was the perfect book for someone who had studied the Holocaust.

About six months later Sara returned the book; I had chosen well. Now I had another book for her: *The Light Between Oceans* by M.L. Stedman, a love story that is ocean deep. I was sure it would interest her. Once again I sent her off without taking any payment for the book, and to my delight she accepted. I love the challenge of choosing the *right* book for a customer to read, and having the freedom to give my books away if I want to. My books find incredible homes.

I also keep a few separate shelves of 'holiday reading' — fiction paperbacks for sale at modest prices that I sometimes lend to my regular readers who go through at least a book a week. They drop a donation into the collection box for Blind Low Vision NZ. Each year we raise around $600.

A few months later Sara came back to return the book (which she loved), and stated very clearly that this time she was going to *buy* a book! I suggested *Where the Crawdads Sing* by Delia Owens, a bestseller and Goodreads award-winner that has been made into a movie.

I didn't see Sara again until I was invited to speak at the Queenstown Writers Festival about my own book. It turned out Sara was going to be my interviewer! When she came to visit me so we could prepare for the event, she told me the biggest news: she had a dog!

Gypsy is Sara's first dog. She had always wanted one, so when they bought their own home Harlan fenced the property and Sara started to look for a rescue dog. A friend of a friend's spaniel-labrador mix was pregnant to a collie working dog, so she suggested that Sara could have one of the puppies when they were born. Sara chose a female with long white socks, brown eyebrows and a black coat. She wanted to call her Colorado — Collie for short — but Gypsy seemed a better fit for this wee bundle of joy. But of course a Cambridge graduate had to give her puppy an elaborate name, so she is actually Colorado Gypsy Johnson, Gypsy for short.

An excited Sara went to collect Gypsy when she was seven weeks old, but on the ride home Gypsy began howling. Sara was distraught, and halfway home she pulled over to the side of the road and the two of them sat together and cried. It was not quite the idyllic beginning Sara had hoped for.

Gypsy soon settled in well, but the next week New Zealand went into Covid lockdown. Harlan and Sara had bought a nice kennel for Gypsy, as she was going to be an outside dog, but, like so many other dogs at that time, she soon came to sleep at the foot of their bed.

But lockdown meant that Sara couldn't take her to puppy school, and there were no playdates with other puppies, so valuable weeks of puppyhood were going by with no formal learning or training for Gypsy, and no guidance for the new parents.

Then Sara discovered Puppy Zen, a virtual puppy school run by Mark Vette. This course offered plenty of guidance, along with a Facebook group to support new puppy owners. Sara signed up and, being the dedicated student she is, soaked up all the information about the importance of eye contact, how to make your puppy wait for food, how to deal with the effects of Covid on dogs and so much more.

To help with socialisation, Sara and Harlan and the two friends they had staying during lockdown would dress up in ski gear so Gypsy would be exposed to other types of clothing. They took turns taking her out walking to see the world. Sara regularly logged onto the Facebook page to share concerns and discuss progress with other members; some of her classmates were going through a horrific time because of lockdown.

During this time Sara was freelance book editing and working in digital marketing, both of which she could do from home. Looking back, she said having Gypsy really helped her get through lockdown, reminding her to make time to play. Sara realised her growing relationship with Gypsy was teaching her the meaning of unconditional love. Sitting straight and still, with head raised, Gypsy looked deeply into Sara's eyes. I am here for you. Are you here for me? And the answer was yes.

It has been a revelation for Sara.

'You want it to be true that the relationships you build in life will be lasting, but often this isn't the case,' she said to me. 'When you forge a relationship with a dog it's long term, you're committed for a lifetime. There is a duty of care, a bond that can withstand anything.'

Sara sighed. 'I need her more than she needs me. Gypsy

gives me more than I can give her; it's the total faith she
has in me. She believes that what I do and say is the best
for her. Tell your dog to get in the car, walk beside you, and
they do — it's a blind trust. Leave them for five minutes
and when they see you again, they're ecstatic. It's beyond
anything to be gifted so much love.'

Lately Sara has been training for a half-marathon with
Gypsy as her pace-setter; Gypsy runs 10 metres ahead and
then waits until Sara catches up. She motivates Sara to get
outside every day. Together with Harlan they go on big
adventures — camping, mountain biking and tramping.
Gypsy has her own sleeping bag, an old featherdown jacket,
and a dog Swanndri. When she was little they carried her
in a backpack but now she has her own trail-running pack
— a vest with side pockets for treats, a water bottle and a
collapsible dish. It matches Sara's backpack; they are a team.

Harlan is an arborist who runs his own business, and
as he often takes Gypsy to work, his mother has made her
a high-vis vest. Gypsy is employed as a supervisor and is
paid a dollar a day.

They often used to bike across the reserve to see a
friend who has a dog called Boy. Gypsy took an immense
liking to Boy and, unbeknown to Sara and Harlan, Gypsy
started taking herself off to visit him. If he wasn't there,
she returned home, only to try again another day. It wasn't
until their friend told them that Gypsy was under the
impression she had solo visiting rights that they realised

she was sneaking out to see her boyfriend.

They had to put a stop to the random visits as it was dangerous for Gypsy to make the journey alone. Gypsy knew she was in trouble when Sara and Harlan turned up at Boy's place one day to pick her up. A quiet but prolonged stay in their enclosed front yard ensured that she knew her secret excursions had come to an end.

Boy and his owner have now moved, but Gypsy still has lots of friends in town she gets to play with — as long as her owner is there!

HUNZA — THE FIRST
BOOKSHOP DOG

—

HUNZA RELUCTANTLY STOPPED being a youth worker when I resigned from my position in 1989. I was completely burnt out. Lance had left the Department of Conservation after 12 years as skipper of the *Renown*, his politics having become too green to fit with DOC's mission.

He was always happiest at sea — he even looked like a man of the sea in his skipper's cap made from showerproof navy wool. During his years with DOC he had gained an incredible amount of scientific knowledge about the underwater world of Fiordland, a place he loves passionately. Fiordland is his cornerstone of life; he calls it his church and has fought to protect it ever since.

We realised that between us we had every ingredient needed to start a charter-boat business with a focus on environmental education. Lance had been a diver for many years, involved in many facets of research. This was how he became aware of the decline in fish stocks, due not only to recreational and commercial overfishing but also to the rapid increase in the number of charter fishing boats.

In August 1985 marine scientist Ken Grange published a paper titled *New Zealand's Southern Fiords: A Marine Wonderland*. For the first time there was scientific evidence that the fiords' underwater habitat was unique in the world. Beneath the waterline, the mountains continue down as a steep rock wall until they reach the flat floor of the fiord, at depths ranging from 100 to more than 450 metres in the deep basins. The region's extremely high rainfall makes for an unequalled amount of freshwater runoff, which sits on top of the salt water forming a dark overlay, blocking out the sun and light.

The resulting darkness creates a habitat between 5 and 40 metres deep that was found to support extremely diverse communities. Scientists found very rare deep-water species including ancient brachiopods, deep-water sponges, large tube anemones, sea pens, soft corals, black coral colonies and over 50 species of fish living relatively near the surface, all tucked closely together forming a kaleidoscope of colour.

In 1978 an Order in Council had removed the fiords from Fiordland National Park, thereby removing their protection. After publication of the 1985 research, scientists realised the importance of re-establishing protection for this important and unique environment.

Lance, having assisted in this research, became a strong advocate for the region's protection. We decided to start a charter-boat business dedicated to the protection of our underwater world. There would be no fishing on board; our focus would be on environmental education to promote conservation, and once we started to make a profit we would support scientific research. Under no circumstances would we compromise our values.

Our accountant and lawyer both thought we were mad — everyone who came to Fiordland, they argued, wanted to go fishing. But our minds were made up and eventually they both supported us. We were totally convinced it would work.

We initially leased the *Evohe*, an 83-foot (25-metre) yacht we had both crewed on for Earth Trust a few years earlier, protesting against the use of drift nets in the Pacific and Tasman oceans. Lance knew the *Evohe* would get a Class 8 survey, a marine standard that would permit us to work not only coastal New Zealand but also down to the subantarctic islands — the Aucklands, Campbells and Antipodes. In 1995 we started operating under the name Fiordland Ecology Holidays.

My 'office' was our small spare bedroom, so Hunza, now aged seven, was with me every day, totally bored after his busy, exciting life in Invercargill, followed by a few years of youth work in Te Anau. I knew he was missing it — missing being idolised and adored by so many people. He had been their hero. Now he was suddenly in early retirement.

He learnt very quickly that a long walk in the morning and another one at night was his exercise for the day, as while Lance was running multi-day trips on the coast I was getting the business side up and running. This was before internet and cellphones, so correspondence was by fax or snail-mail. It wasn't until about a year later that I bought my first computer and printer.

Hunza loved the days when clients would come to check in with me the day before a trip departure. Extra people around meant numerous opportunities for attention, and at times it was as though he wanted to hold a full conversation. He would sit just in front of a person, ears pricked, back straight, eyes locked on theirs and just stare. At the very least he received pats on the head or a rub behind the ears, and occasionally someone did talk to him. His response was instant, cocking his head on the side, mouth slightly open. If the conversation went on, he would stand up and in his own way become totally involved.

I have always talked to my pets. It's usually only one or two basic sentences — 'How are you today?' or 'What have you been up to?' being the standard opening gambits. But when Lance was away for days at a time and it was only me and Hunza at home — going for walks, working in the office, then at night having dinner — we began having extremely complex conversations.

Lance and I had put everything on the line to start our charter business. The budget was calculated down to the last cent — even how much we needed for Hunza's food and vet bills. For a little additional income we ran a bed-and-breakfast in the fully self-contained flat that has a common wall with our place. It was only $60 a night but this was my home money, and every little bit helped.

Our meals were very basic and Hunza was down to having Weet-Bix or porridge for breakfast, sometimes with a slice of toast, and for dinner mashed vegetables and gravy, or just rice and an egg. We ate the same thing every day, sitting together and talking. The highlight was when Lance came home after a trip, bringing with him any food left over — fruit, vegetables, bread and sometimes meat. I was, and still am, a vegetarian, so the meat went to Hunza. What a joy that was.

Hunza took it upon himself to go visiting around Manapōuri, dropping in to see people who gave him snacks, and even stealing other cats' and dogs' meals. I didn't know about this until a woman from around the corner came to tell me that Hunza kept stealing her dog's dinner. I was extremely embarrassed.

That night when we sat down together Hunza knew there was something wrong, as I was crying. His eyes were so sad, his ears were flat and he whimpered quietly. I told him he would have to be with me or tied up all the time — no more wandering around our small township. Times were tough and we needed to work together as he was an incredibly important part of our team. He kept me sane through that time — even when I was exhausted we went for walks. We talked continually, and often fell asleep wrapped around each other on the floor.

I was going to the Baptist church at that time and the minister, Peter Appleton, was also a close friend. He once organised a food box for us that included tinned dog food. It was like Christmas! Hunza sensed the excitement and joined in, jumping up and down, half barking and half howling, his tail wagging as I unpacked the box and told him in detail about all the wonderful yummies.

After about a year we rented a small holiday home that became the official office of Fiordland Ecology Holidays, and also the birthplace of 45 South and Below Bookshop, which began with fewer than 100 books.

Hunza became the first bookshop dog.

HANK

HANDSOME HANK

Hank walked past the bookshops on a lead, striding confidently beside Chris, head held high. Hank is a massive German shepherd, weighing in at 43 kg. I called out to Chris and asked to be introduced. Hank, big and black, with massive paws, seemed to smile as he came over to me and waited for a pat. He leaned in towards me, making sure he had my full attention.

After that initial introduction I often saw Hank at the bookshop with Chris and Anne, and as usual I welcomed Hank well before his owners, maybe because they didn't run towards me seeking a pat.

Hank lived his first three years with a family who broke up and, as neither partner could keep him, they offered him free to a good home on Trade Me. This was in August 2020. Chris and Anne had just lost their previous German shepherd, Chip, to cancer at 12 years old and desperately wanted another. They started looking and there was Hank, but many people were chasing after him and his owner was being very thorough in her quest to find Hank the right home. All prospective owners were extensively quizzed and Chris and Anne were one of two families who made the shortlist.

It was arranged that both families would go and meet Hank and his owners, one in the morning, and the other in the afternoon. To her credit, the owner was taking every possible step to ensure Hank went to the right family. Chris and Anne were sitting quietly on the deck watching Hank play in the garden when, without any encouragement, Hank went over to Chris and dropped his head on his knee. They both patted him, played with him, and fell in love with him, knowing all the time he wasn't yet theirs.

As they were driving back to Invercargill their cellphone rang. With considerable apprehension Chris answered, and was ecstatic to be told that Hank was theirs.

'What made you choose us?' Chris asked.

'He chose you when he put his head on your knee,' the woman replied.

Two weeks later they picked Hank up and took him home to begin the settling-in period. Then, two days after Hank's arrival, Chris had a heart attack and was rushed to hospital. It was an understandably unsettling time for them all, but by the time Chris came home from hospital Hank was well ensconced. From then, he quickly became Chris's dog.

Living in a semi-rural area meant Hank had a big playground, and having him around gave the family peace of mind, especially when Chris was away working.

One of Chris and Anne's granddaughters had had a traumatic experience with a big dog when she was only two. Her grandparents were concerned that she might be scared of 'big Hank', so they were very careful in introducing him to his extended family. They shared photos and video clips of him first, and told them stories about how gentle he was and how he loved to play. When the family came down from Christchurch for a holiday the grandchildren already knew Hank was big. But *this* big?!

Hank stayed outside at first so the girls could watch him through the sliding glass door. He was about the same height as the youngest granddaughter, so they were looking directly into each other's eyes. It quickly seemed as though there was an understanding between them, because when the door was opened, Hank walked inside the house and just sat down. In his gentle way he wove his way into the wee girl's heart.

Like most dogs, Hank loves to swim, and spends countless hours fetching sticks thrown into the nearby river. He is a regular feature at the Manapōuri Boating Club ramp, where he swims between the comings and goings of boats — regardless of the weather.

His first ball was a large leather soccer ball, which he enthusiastically punctured and tore to shreds in a few minutes. After doing some research, Chris bought an indestructible ball that was being marketed as the *Titanic* of all balls . . . Hank soon learnt that he couldn't get his teeth into it, no matter hard he tried, but he was determined to move it somehow. So he punched it with his front paw, and from that time on he started to dribble the ball like a soccer player.

Handsome Hank has found a great home with Chris and Anne.

Berri

BERRI THE BEAUTIFUL

B erri is named after the actress Halle Berry, but Phil, her owner, liked the idea of spelling it a little differently. The connection was obvious to Phil because his dog was so beautiful, with bright colouring, sparkly eyes and a captivating personality. Berri is a Staffordshire bull terrier cross: medium build, quite muscular, very gentle, highly inquisitive and extremely affectionate. The only Staffie giveaway is the white diamond on her chest.

In 2009 a brief advertisement in the *Southland Times* had caught Phil's eye: 'Dog, free to good home.' He rang the number and learnt that the puppy's mother had abandoned her as she didn't have enough milk to feed the whole litter. She was only seven weeks old and was being hand-fed.

Initially she was very, *very* demanding, and needed constant company. She howled when left alone. Phil nearly gave her back but she was so adorable he couldn't bring himself to part with her. After two traumatic weeks she started to settle down, but then the howling was replaced by other antisocial behaviour...

She was left by herself in the house for eight hours each day when Phil went to work, and clearly she didn't like that arrangement. Berri literally ate two sofas, chewed the legs of the dining suite and chairs, tried to eat the bottom layer of the bed and even attacked the wallpaper in the hallway. Phil is a kind soul with a forgiving nature so he put up with the progressive destruction of his home. He really wanted to keep her, and felt he needed to. Who else would put up with her? Finally she settled and her destructive streak was replaced by her total commitment to Phil.

When she was about seven years old Phil adopted Paddy, a black and tan huntaway cross. Paddy belonged to a friend who was moving and could not take Paddy with him. Phil had met his friend's dog a couple of times and liked him a lot, so the decision to adopt him was easy. Paddy quickly established with Berri that he was the alpha dog and then, that issue sorted, the two dogs became good friends.

Tehimana, known to everyone as Des, moved into our small cottage overlooking the lake some years ago. He is a flax weaver and gardener, and is passionate about promoting Māori culture and tikanga. When Des came into Phil's life Paddy was initially apprehensive, but after a short time Paddy and Berri grew attached to him.

A few years ago Paddy developed a lump on his left thigh that proved to be cancerous. He had surgery but the cancer spread into his groin and they decided to have him put down. After a last special weekend together in Te Anau, one of Paddy's favourite places, Des and Phil took him to the vet. Berri went with them but she was aloof and distant, as if she knew what was going to happen and had already accepted that her best friend was leaving her. Phil believes that Berri knew what was going on and was already going through the grieving process.

Now Berri lives for most of the year in Invercargill with Phil, and visits Manapōuri frequently when he comes up to stay with his partner, Des. She has the best of both worlds. Her love — after Phil and Des — is our beautiful Lake Manapōuri.

Phil, now retired, recently spent three years studying te reo Māori through Te Wānanga o Aotearoa at the Southland Institute of Technology. He had always wanted to learn the language and now he has finally fulfilled his wish. He was the oldest in the class by quite a few years and although he found some of the course difficult, he is proud of what he has achieved.

Phil loves my Wee Bookshops. In fact Lance and I left him in charge over Easter 2022 and took a little holiday. We spent a few hours familiarising him, and I told him to open the shops around 10.30 a.m. and close whenever he wanted. I thought the Easter trade would be quiet as New Zealand's borders were still closed because of Covid.

When we returned from our six-day break I found Phil happy but exhausted. The bookshops had been incredibly busy — the Saturday had been our best sales day ever! Sunday and Monday had also been busy so Phil had kept the shop open longer.

Des had even set up a weaving table on the grass beside the shops to entertain customers as they waited to get into the shops. Vicky, my friend who owns the second-hand shop Time Traders, just around the corner, delivered coffee to Phil to keep him going, and Des brought him food!

Phil proudly took me into the shops where I was greeted with half-empty shelves — the Children's Bookshop was nearly bare. For weeks after, my regulars told me how wonderful he had been. I should have known that the man who tolerated having his home methodically destroyed by his dog because of a deep love, would be the perfect person to look after my bookshops. He had clearly been in his element.

Berri is now nearly 14 years old, her once-bright colours now dulled with grey. Her eyes are an old dog's eyes but they still sparkle and are full of mischief. She thinks she owns the beach down at the lake; she prefers the front seat of the car; the sofa is hers; the bed is hers; and she owns Phil and Des.

She has woven her way perfectly into Phil and Des's lives, using only the best flax fibre with silk-like texture. Like Des, she has ensured that her pattern was woven with love and will therefore withstand the passing of time when she has gone from their lives.

HUNZA AND THE HEDGEHOG

—

WHY WAS HUNZA attracted to the small prickly hedgehogs that visited our garden?

Maybe it was their shape, since when they curl up tightly, surrounding themselves with sharp quills for protection, they look like a ball. Or was it just curiosity? A dog sees a small animal shuffling over the lawn, and then in an instant it turns into a ball — that's pretty amazing. Who wouldn't want to investigate?

One afternoon we noticed that Hunza had a number of pinpricks on the bridge of his nose. The area looked a little red but nothing much to worry about.

By the following morning, things were much worse. The bridge of Hunza's nose was now swollen, red and oozing, and several more small puncture marks were visible. He was still his happy self but we could tell his nose was starting to bother him as he was rubbing it constantly with his paw. Time to take him to the vet.

The vet immediately identified an infection from a hedgehog, which would continue to spread if it wasn't treated. And unfortunately, he told us, in many cases this was difficult to achieve. We started Hunza on antibiotics and an ointment, but the infection kept spreading. After a couple of weeks it was getting towards his eyes, so in desperation I took him to a vet in Invercargill who specialised in dogs. He was worried that Hunza would transfer the infection to other parts of his body through licking, and sent poor Hunza back to Manapōuri with a bucket on his head.

Lance was away at sea but wanted me to keep him updated on Hunza's progress. This wasn't easy, as we didn't have a satellite phone on board *Breaksea Girl*. But we did have a marine radio base set up in our kitchen so I could contact Lance at least a couple of times a day, and also listen in to marine weather forecasts. I had to radio him from our single sideband marine radio, which meant our communication could be heard by vessels all over New Zealand who were tuned in to 4417 MHz.

'*Breaksea Girl, Breaksea Girl*, do you copy, Lance?'

'Copy, Ruth.'

'I have an update on Hunza.'

'Okay, go ahead.'

'Hunza has a bucket on his head to stop him licking his testicles.'

Lance couldn't quite believe what I had just broadcast. There was a short silence before he replied, 'Can you please repeat that.'

I repeated clearly, 'Hunza has a bucket on his head to stop him licking his testicles as the infection can be easily spread.'

I heard laughter as Lance tried to control himself, before saying, 'I understand now. I thought you said Hunter. You mean Hunza — Hotel, Uniform, November, Zulu, Alpha.'

'Yes,' I replied. 'Hunza.'

Hunter was Lance's older brother, hence the unfortunate misunderstanding. It doesn't bear thinking about, really.

The radio waves were silent as dozens of mariners tried to unravel our conversation. We thought it incredibly funny but I have to say that when we told Hunter his reaction was a stunned silence. Thankfully he did laugh in the end.

When Lance came home, Hunza's hedgehog infection was still progressing and it was now up over one eye. Lance had learnt as a child that a natural remedy against stinging nettle was to use the juice of the dock leaf, *Rumex obtusifolius*. He heated some leaves in a saucepan, then squeezed them to extract the juice. He then combined the juice with the crushed leaf to use it as a poultice. To hold the poultice in place we placed a stocking over Hunza's snout. He looked pretty strange but in his usual placid way he just ignored it. Over the next few days the infection started to clear. The bridge of his nose was permanently left with lines of shallow scars.

Rumex obtusifolius: Dock can often be found growing near stinging nettle, and its leaves are used in many cultures to soothe nettle stings. The cooling properties are also used to soothe insect bites and stings, as well as scalds, blisters and sprains.

Lucy & Eliza

THE CHEMIST'S CANINES

George, our local chemist in Te Anau, is an Englishman from a small town called Swanley, just out of London. He had just graduated as a pharmacist when he came to New Zealand on a six-month holiday and decided to stay. When he began work at the Te Anau Pharmacy he met co-worker Michelle: beautiful, blonde and highly competent.

The two married in 2008, when Michelle's children were aged between 10 and 16. They decided they would buy the pharmacy, and, as though that wasn't stressful enough, they acquired a puppy just two days prior to their grand opening. They heard of a litter of labrador puppies being given away, and decided that if there was a yellow female they would take her.

And there she was, a fat wee golden girl. Not a pure bred, but oh! so beautiful! George had planned to ask the owners to keep her for another two weeks to give them time to settle into their new business, but on seeing her, he couldn't resist. 'Let's take her home now!'

Sophie was supposed to be an outside dog but, like so many dogs, she quickly made it known that she was an inside one. After only a few hours on her first day she progressed from the garage to the lounge, then into the bedroom, and when she still cried, she was finally allowed to snuggle up in their bed. George and Michelle were so busy with their new chemist shop that they basically let Sophie do what she wanted. Puppy bliss! It took a couple of weeks to establish some ground rules.

When Sophie was seven years old a friend visited the pharmacy with their spoodle named Poppy. Both Michelle and George adored her. They contacted the breeder in the North Island, handed over $1500 (which they thought was a *lot* of money) and became the devoted owners of a female puppy they named Eliza. She is named after Eliza Thornberry from the English cartoon *The Wild Thornberrys*, hence her nickname, Thorny. This was before the breed became 'Instagramable' and the price increased to around $5000!

Sophie was 15 when she developed a tumour inside her nose that started to bleed. She kept sneezing and rubbing her nose on the ground as it was so uncomfortable. Over a very short time the tumour must have spread to her brain as she began to experience fits, which became quite violent. George and Michelle knew a hard decision had to be made. Then one day Michelle was at home with Sophie when her eyes went dull, she started drooling copiously and then had a massive fit. It was time to say goodbye.

Because of Covid the vet couldn't come to their home, so they placed Sophie on her bed in the large boot of their car and drove her to town. She looked happy, as going for a ride in the car always meant an adventure. The vet put her to sleep while she lay on her bed. George and Michelle had thought they would be able to hold her and say their final farewells, but she slipped into unconsciousness immediately. They returned home devastated and couldn't talk about it for weeks.

Eliza, who was now six years old, took the loss of her best friend Sophie extremely hard. She started to howl continually, so loudly that neighbours nearly 2 kilometres away rang to ask George what was happening.

As no amount of love and cuddles seemed able to stop Eliza from being distressed, they decided to get another puppy to keep her company. Eliza is a highly strung spoodle so they decided a laid-back labradoodle might have a calming influence.

They drove for over four hours to visit a respected labradoodle breeder in Dunback and came home with Lucy (though George calls her Goose because it's easier to shout when she's naughty).

George owns a 70-year-old Ferguson TEA tractor on which he delights in carrying out challenging jobs around their property. Moving a 250-kilogram chicken run on a 25-degree slope when the hydraulics were faulty is only one of his memorable adventures. When he was shifting a load of wet wood weighing approximately 450 kg he blew a gasket, covering himself in hydraulic oil. Quick on-site repairs had him underway again — for a short time.

Just prior to the photoshoot for this book, Michelle had to tow George on his tractor out into the paddock when he couldn't it started. George eventually found there was water running down one side of the engine, and the thermostat housing on top of the radiator had corroded and blown open. He got it up and running again and was proudly showing his friend John what had happened when the fan (which is belt driven) hit his hand and he nearly lost his knuckles. (Latest information is that the tractor is up and running again — for now — and George's hand has healed.)

I'm not convinced George should even own a tractor, but you can tell from his big smile when he regales us with his tractor stories that he is certainly having a lot of fun. The saga continues . . .

George likes to read but has little time, what with running his very busy pharmacy (and fixing his tractor). Whenever I get a book in that I think he may enjoy I drop it off to him. *A Short History of Tractors in Ukrainian* by Marina Lewycka was a must-read for him.

George grew up with dogs and finds them a great comfort. Sparrows and blackbirds also remind him of home.

As we chat, the dogs are asleep, Eliza snoring softly as George rubs her tummy, Lucy stretched out in front of the fire. They have their own dog room built on one corner of the house, but what luxury to be inside on a winter's night with George and Michelle.

George admits that he constantly thinks about the dogs when he is at work; he frets when he is away from them as they are such a huge part of his life. Michelle smiles. She has been a mother so she understands how George feels. Like so many other dog owners, they cannot imagine what it would be like not to have a dog — or two — in the family.

YOU WERE NEVER JUST HUNZA

—

HUNZA WAS READY for his afternoon walk and run along the lake shore, staring up at me while I gathered his lead and pulled my hat on. It's only a short walk from our place to the lake, but it always took time as Hunza sniffed all his regular spots to check out what other dogs had been in the area. I noticed he was a little slower than usual. He usually ran ahead of me but today it was just a slow trot, and his tail was hanging low. As we walked down onto the beach Hunza cocked his leg up against a large rock and I noticed that his urine was bright red.

Hardly believing what I had seen — and not wanting to think about what it meant — I told him to sit and stay, as I needed to run back home to get the car. I was crying when I pulled up on the road across from where Hunza was sitting waiting for me. He looked fine, but I knew he wasn't. I had to lift him into the back seat of the car as he couldn't jump. He lay down and closed his eyes. Lance was away at sea so I was on my own.

Thankfully, the road between Manapōuri and Te Anau is nearly always quiet so I drove fast, ignoring the speed limit. As I drove the 20 kilometres I continually talked to Hunza.

Thinking back, it was as though I was trying to convince myself as well as him that everything would be all right. I pulled up outside the back door of the vet's, raced in without knocking and called for Brian.

Within minutes he was lifting Hunza out of the car. As he carried him into the surgery Hunza lifted his head and looked at me, his beautiful brown eyes locked onto mine. I tried to smile and whispered something stupid like, 'It's all right, you're going to be fine.' Brian laid him on the table and felt his abdomen. Then he injected him with a painkiller and inserted a catheter. Blood drained quickly, filling the bowl.

Brian turned to me.

'Ruth, he has a very swollen abdomen, which is still tight even after I have taken off so much blood. He is bleeding internally. I can either operate immediately to see what is happening, or I can put him to sleep.'

I was stunned. This was all so quick. I stood quietly, one hand on Hunza's head while the other stroked his soft body. I was shaking, tears running down my face and dripping onto my coat.

Brian placed a hand over mine. 'It's your decision, Ruth.' He turned and left.

Hunza was asleep, his breathing deep and slow. Did he know when he looked at me as he was being carried in here that this was the end? Or was he confident that I would make the right decision? How does anyone make this decision when everything happens so suddenly?

This morning there was no sign of sickness, and he was only nine years old!

I felt his warmth under my hand, the steady heartbeat, and then watched as blood continued to drip into the bowl on the floor. Hunza, my best friend, my playmate and work companion, at times my pathway back to sanity. What was the right decision? What was best for Hunza?

Brian returned, briefly looked at me and then continued to examine his patient.

'I think it would be best to let him go,' he said softly.

Had he felt something? Did he know what was wrong but wasn't telling me because I was already so upset? I couldn't believe this was happening, that this was how Hunza would leave us. Only an hour ago we were getting ready to go for a walk and he was the happy, adventurous Hunza, the dog who accepted everyone, the dog who had helped so many through tough times, and the dog everyone loved.

I folded my arms around him and laid my head close to his. I wasn't crying, I was sobbing, gasping for breath. I wanted to scream, 'Hunza, Hunza!' to bring him back. I was drowning in the love I had for him.

'Put him to sleep,' I said.

Brian was gentle and the end came quickly. Hunza's paws moved slightly, and then nothing.

I asked the vet to ring Peter, our church minister, as I wanted someone who knew not only me but also Hunza, to help me bury him in our back yard. Peter came straight away. He carried Hunza back out to the car, and in his understanding way helped me piece myself back together. We dug his grave, lined it with fronds of ferns and laid our loyal, beautiful friend down. After covering him with more ferns we said our final goodbyes.

Lance came home the next day to the devastating news. We stood silently, holding hands, not believing Hunza was gone. The runt of the litter who had helped stitch back together so many lives. He was never just Hunza.

I remembered his first 'intervention' when I was a youth worker, when the mother hugged her young son and whispered to Hunza, 'Thank you, thank you, thank you, you precious dog.'

Even now, so many years later, we keep calling other dogs Hunza by mistake, for no other reason than that we continually miss him. He is still with us in so many ways.

S.I.D.

SID THE BIRDWATCHER

When I had my first bookshop, 45 South and Below in the late 1990s, Mark was new to collecting books. He was a crayfisherman on the Fiordland coast for many years, then in his forties he sold his boat. Mark's semi-retirement plan was to build an upmarket lodge, hence his interest in books: he wanted a top-quality library.

Dougal, his golden labrador and master digger, always met me at the front door when I went to visit. When searching for rabbits, nothing deterred Dougal from the job in hand. He was once found with only his tail sticking out of the massive hole he had dug chasing his prey. Dougal was only about eight years old when he developed cancer of the jaw and had to be put down.

I invited Mark to accompany me to Dunedin to attend a book auction run by Pam Plumbly. We left Manapōuri at 5.30 a.m. for the three-and-a-half-hour drive. I wanted to be at the auction room at least an hour early so we could go through the books and pencil prices in our catalogues.

I gave Mark a few tips on bidding and price estimates for the books he wanted to buy. I circled the books I wanted in his catalogue, and we agreed not to bid against each other.

The auction starts and bidding is strong among the gathered book dealers and collectors. Mark is eager, too eager — he can't keep still. The first lot he wants comes up. Pam has hardly finished describing the book when Mark throws his arm straight up in the air. There's another bid, and another. Mark says nothing, just keeps his arm stiffly upright until all other bidders fall silent.

He has won his first book.

Buyers turn to look at him. Who is this new guy on the block? Mark now has the buyer's bug — I can almost see it crawling all over him. With a massive smile he whispers, 'I'm going to win the next book — watch me.'

'I don't want to, Mark!' I protest. 'Try and stay within the estimates we wrote down. Don't overbid!'

He smiles, clearly planning to completely ignore my advice. 'This is fun!'

I shake my head, realising it is quite useless trying to rein him in. We both laugh, disturbing the quiet of the room. When another book comes up that Mark wants, he employs his stiff-arm strategy once more. Other bidders turn to look at him, and I am sure that when they see his upright arm they stop bidding. This man has no limits.

Mark bought every book he had wanted, plus a lot more.

I had a scary but very funny vision of the front page of the next day's *Otago Daily Times*: 'Book prices soar at Plumbly's auction'. Or 'Books, the new investment'.

Now, years later, Mark has an extensive library but he didn't ever build the lodge. He fell in love with a Swiss woman he met when she was holidaying in New Zealand, and they eventually married and moved to Nelson. We kept in touch, Mark emailing me for information on books and occasionally buying one.

When Lance and I headed up to Nelson on my book tour, I suggested to Mark that we drop in to see them. He emailed straight back: 'Have bed with ensuite, come and stay.' This was followed by several more emails: Carol made incredible bread, they had a spa bath, they made excellent vegetarian meals and I needed to see his library. Then the clincher: they had a dog! Okay, we would love to stay the night.

Sid, a German wirehaired pointer, came from the small Southland town of Tūātapere. When they picked him up from the airport Mark had decided he was going to travel on the back of the truck, because 'all dogs should travel in the back of a truck'. This lasted about a minute, and the puppy came home warmly nestled in Carol's lap.

They didn't name him for a long time as nothing seemed to suit him — until they tried Sid. It sounded right, and fitted him perfectly. Who would call a gentle, comic-book-looking dog Sid? Well, my friends Mark and Carol did.

When we arrived, Sid welcomed us in his goofy, happy way, his deep brown eyes tucked behind long strands of unruly hair. He was now nine years old.

Of course the conversation initially was all about Sid.

Every morning Mark and Sid walk up the road before the first light of day. One morning Sid stopped, pointed at a tree and absolutely wouldn't budge. Mark began searching the branches with his torch and eventually found what Sid was pointing at — a morepork. A few weeks later Sid stopped and pointed out another morepork sitting quietly in a tree on their driveway. They have been on bike rides when Sid has become so locked in to his point that they have had to go back to him and physically turn him around 90 degrees to get him to snap out of it. He is classic middle management: he doesn't run after anything, just points.

One summer a weka had hatched a large number of chicks close to their house. Having finished his breakfast, Sid was lying down on his beanbag enjoying the sunshine. Suddenly baby weka were running back and forth over his beanbag just a few centimetres from his head. In a flash they ran to his bowl, where their mother was feeding them his leftover breakfast. Sid stared at them in disbelief but never moved a muscle. The audacity!

I lay in bed that night and decided the name Sid actually stood for Specialist Indicating Dog, as that is what he does with no training at all.

cove

COVE THE BOOKSHOP DOG

We had been dogless since Hunza died 19 years earlier. Before Cove's first stay with us, his owner Regan dropped off a dog bed, a soft toy rabbit, a huge bucket of dog food, bones for the freezer, a collar and lead, and Cove's rain jacket. Regan's father Phil had the exact same dog paraphernalia at his place, so wherever Cove stays, he has everything set up and ready.

When we opened the first Wee Bookshop, Cove was as excited as I was, though perhaps for different reasons. Our ship's bell was placed near the bookshop door so customers could ring it when they arrive. I can hear it no matter where I am in the house, the garden or in our small forest.

Cove learnt very quickly that when the bell rang it meant people had arrived to greet him and give him lots of love. He became the self-appointed Bookshop Dog from that time on, eagerly on duty from opening time until close. He can never get enough pats — long, slow strokes along his back, rubs behind the ears — from customers happy to confirm how wonderful he is. When mail and presents started to arrive addressed to 'Cove, Two Wee Bookshops, Manapōuri', I knew he had made his presence felt.

He unashamedly lies down at a customer's feet, rolls onto his back, exposing all his male attributes, and looks up with pleading eyes. 'Oh, isn't he adorable' is one of the frequent comments. As though that isn't enough, he follows customers into the shop, leans up against their legs and gazes up at them for more attention. He then follows them out to their car and with total confidence silently suggests that he should hop in. 'Oh look, he wants to come with us. Isn't that cute?'

A few years ago, over a period of a month, we noticed Cove was getting constipated, and it became severe. He was on medication but required several trips to the vet for an enema. He was taken to a small outer room where the concrete floor sloped down to a drain hole. Cove stood near the drain hole quietly, submitting to the procedure with ears flattened. As soon as the vet stepped away from him, Cove turned and raced out around to the back of the surgery where he squatted, his face registering a look of utter relief. He wasn't standing inside with us to await the results of the bowel flushing, he was hell bent on racing outside to find an area that offered him some privacy. After the first bowel cleanout I left him alone, as he had made it very clear that this was not an event that required an audience.

A few weeks later he was still having problems. Regan turned up with Cove one Friday just after dinner, saying he was very concerned about him. Cove sat down by the fire, head drooped and nearly touching the carpet, hardly moving.

'He needs to go back to the vet, Regan,' I said. There had been no improvement — in fact his health was deteriorating. Now he had started to vomit occasionally.

Regan rang the vet and it was decided that Cove was having a reaction to his new medication. He took him straight to see the vet in Te Anau and returned around midnight.

The next morning Regan rang the vet to report that Cove was trying to poo but was in obvious pain. The vet said a scan was required, in either Dunedin or Christchurch. Christchurch was the better option for Regan as his sister lived there. He made an appointment for the Tuesday, and set out on Monday for the eight-hour drive.

The scan showed multiple cysts on the prostate and arthritis in the lower spine. Plus he had a bladder infection.

The next day, Cove underwent major surgery. Over the following week he was in recovery, monitored 24 hours a day at the After Hours Veterinary Clinic. Regan spent many hours at his side and was grateful that the experienced staff were so caring.

All up, the bill came to just under $10,000, hence Cove's new nickname, 'The Million Dollar Dog'.

When Regan brought Cove back we had to manage a few post-op problems, which resolved themselves over time. He had also become slightly incontinent, so small trickles of urine would sprinkle the pathway as he walked, but this is now managed through medication.

Cove just accepts whatever is happening. He's a dog who fits in and makes allowances. When I was raising Katherine Mansfield, the baby thrush, he would watch me intently as I hand-fed her, and when she started to embark on short, uncertain flights across the room he sat and followed her progress with interest. She once landed on him and he didn't move, not even when she hopped across his body to find a cosy place to sit.

At the ripe old age of 15 he has become very protective of *his* three bookshops, and is sometimes disapproving of any other dogs who visit. When this happens I walk him back to the house and close him inside until the visiting dog has gone. The look he gives me is unbelievable, but he reluctantly accepts what is required of him.

His front paws are now splayed, he is totally deaf, he frequently limps, he has noticeable cataracts, and his twice-daily walks now consist of sniffing, peeing and plodding. He snores, he farts, he dribbles at mealtimes — he is really showing his age. Not so long ago Cove stood up and walked over to Lance, who was sitting on the couch beside me. His upper cheeks were puffed out, his mouth clamped shut as he stared intently at Lance, not moving.

'Look at Cove,' Lance said to me. 'He's trying to tell me something. What is it, Cove?'

They looked directly at each other for a few minutes, then Cove turned, took a few steps towards the front door and casually dropped a small poo on the carpet.

'Oh, he wanted to go outside! Oh well, too late,' said Lance. 'I won't forget that look now I know what it means.'

We both laughed. Just another sign of Cove growing old. The three or four pills he takes each morning, and the drops of Propalin syrup for his urinary incontinence, are keeping him happy and content for now.

Stella

ALL ABOUT THE DOGS

Sarah and Dave had a dog named Scooba, a German wirehaired pointer, so named because at the time they got her they owned a diving business. They weren't looking for another dog but heard about a couple who were separating and needed to find a home for their five-year-old dog. Sarah and Dave adopted Chalky, named after Chalky Sound, near the southern end of Fiordland. Chalky loved Scooba. When she died a few years later, at the age of 13, he would often be found lying near her grave.

It was not long after this that Stella came on the scene.

Stella had lived in three other homes before she came to Sarah and Dave. The first family relocated to Australia so she was taken back to her breeder, who then found her a new home with a friend of Dave's. Sarah immediately took a liking to Stella. 'Oh, she's gorgeous! If things don't work out in her new home we'll have her!' she said to Dave. Three months later Stella had moved in with Chalky.

Stella is a Hungarian wirehaired Vizsla. She is eight years old going on 18 months, sporting heavily whiskered eyebrows, a small untidy moustache and a 24-hour smile. She always has lots to say as she welcomes anyone, before offering them her soft toy penguin. Stella thinks she is pretty special as there are not many WHVs in New Zealand, and she delights in all the attention. Oh, and do *not* call her red, orange or ginger — she is *russet*, which makes her even more important.

Stella was, and still is, an anxious dog. With her history, perhaps part of her is expecting to be moved on again. With an alley-cat mentality she will pick up anything white, possibly thinking it is fat. Everything from coffee cups to paper and even patches of snow are set upon and devoured. Sarah thinks it is a fixation on survival — she is always searching for food. It took her two years to settle down enough to sleep on her bed rather than in her crate, which offered her security.

Chalky had been with Sarah and Dave for five years when Sarah was diagnosed with breast cancer in 2015. She had surgery a week after her fiftieth birthday. When she came home from the hospital Chalky became her cancer buddy, always there beside her. Because Sarah had Chalky's full attention, Dave felt less anxious about leaving her at home when he went to work for the Department of Conservation in Te Anau. He also occasionally had to go into the fiords to monitor bottle-nosed dolphin populations.

Sarah had a slow recovery but 18 months later she was able to return to work part time. Chalky was getting older and was no longer up for long walks, so Sarah took him on a short walk with Stella each morning. But Stella really needed a long romping walk every day so Sarah suggested that Dave start walking Stella at night. Over a short period Stella turned the walk into a run — their walk around the block had somehow become a 6-km run.

Chalky died at the grand old age of 15, when Stella had been with them for about two years.

Dave and Sarah are keen readers and frequent visitors to my shops. When they drop by Stella stays in the vehicle, head out the window, taking in everything that is going on. One or two members of her dog social circle are nearly always with her and a loud cacophony of barking and whining reminds everyone that they are there, impatiently waiting for their walk.

Dave collects books on Antarctica. Every Christmas and birthday Sarah buys him a special book for his collection, which is now quite extensive.

As Sarah is an avid reader like me, we have established a borrowing/swap system. We both enjoy books that are a little different, such as *Stillicide* by Cynan Jones, which was shortlisted for the Wales Book of the Year Fiction Prize; *The Master Butchers Singing Club* by Louise Erdrich, a Native American novelist, which is about German immigrants adapting to their new life in America; and *Eleanor Oliphant is Completely Fine*, a first novel by Gail Honeyman and winner of the 2017 Costa Debut Novel Award.

I recently came across a fabulous book, *Good Dogs Don't Make it to the South Pole* by Hans-Olav Thyvold. The story is told through the eyes of a dog named Tassen, and is about his relationship with his recently widowed elderly owner. Woven throughout the story is the story of Roald Amundsen's expedition to the South Pole. It's a must-read for any dog lover.

Dave and Sarah always seem to have a houseful of canine visitors. When they speak about any of their dogs their eyes are either full of love and happiness, or full of tears. Dave has a different voice for every dog that comes into their home. (I don't think I have 'advanced' to that level yet!) Their lives really are all about their dogs.

Just before Covid lockdown, Dave was working on the Fiordland coast, staying at the hostel in Deep Cove with two dolphin researchers, Chloe and Will. Deep Cove, at the head of Doubtful Sound, is a rather remote place. To get there you have to cross Lake Manapōuri by boat, then drive over the Wilmot Pass — nearly an hour and a half all up. The only other options are helicopter or float plane.

Dave had earlier spoken to his doctor about a pain between his shoulders and mentioned that he felt uncomfortable when he bent over. He was also experiencing shortness of breath. His father had died young from a heart attack so he was on the alert in case there was a hereditary problem. Medication was prescribed and he was given the all-clear to go over to Doubtful Sound to continue his work.

After dinner in the hostel one night Dave went to stand up and collapsed. His colleague Chloe, knowing Dave's strange sense of humour, thought he was messing around, but it soon became obvious to her and Will that Dave had had a heart attack. They immediately carried out CPR, and Chloe raced to get a defibrillator. Dave came back to life after the second shock from the defibrillator.

Luck was with Dave that night; another man staying at the hostel immediately turned up with an oxygen kit, which was kept in the university laboratory for divers. Dave went immediately from blue to pink. He was then flown by helicopter to Dunedin Hospital, where he spent three weeks recovering before he had a six-way heart bypass. Incredibly, Dave had been the first-aid instructor who had trained Chloe and her team, who were now instrumental in saving his life.

Eventually Dave came home. Much to Stella's delight they were soon back walking and, even better, it was blackberry season so she could munch her favourite berries along the way. It took a few months before Dave was back running but now on alternate days you will see Dave with his headphones on running along with Stella as he listens to *Zombies, Run!*, an interactive running app where players act as the character 'Runner 5', with a series of missions to carry out while they are chased by zombies …

Stella has found the perfect home, surrounded by her many dog friends, and loved enormously by Dave and

Sarah. Her purpose in life is to be loved by everyone, to keep Dave healthy by running away from zombies, and to share as much time as possible with her best friend Maxi, who you are about to meet.

MAXI

MAXI WHO TRIED TO BE GOOD

Maxi is another German wirehaired pointer. He often comes to the bookshops with Sarah, Dave and Stella, his best friend. Maxi also comes in with his owner, who is always on the lookout for books that might interest the passengers on *Breaksea Girl*, which she now owns and operates on the Fiordland coast.

So where did Maxi come from?

When Fi and her partner Brian visited a farm near Ōtautau to look at some puppies, they had no intention of taking one home — but that is exactly what happened. Maxi went with them 'on trial'. The bouncing, long-legged, out-of-control three-month-old won their hearts in short order. He settled in straight away, didn't cry at night, was reasonably well behaved, and responded quickly and intelligently to Brian's training regime. He quickly became a permanent fixture.

Within a few months Maxi had worked his way up to be top dog in this one-dog family. One night just after Fi and

Brian moved into their first home, Maxi made it known that he wanted to go outside for a wee in the middle of the night. Brian got up to let him out and patiently stood on the deck waiting for him to come back. Maxi seemed to be taking a very long time, but Brian continued to wait, unaware that Maxi had sneaked back into the house and hopped into bed with Fi, settling down to sleep in the nice warm space Brian had recently occupied. Eventually Brian gave up waiting and, discovering what had happened, climbed in beside the large snoring dog and accepted that he was no longer top dog.

As a pup Maxi went to work with Fi, who at that time was managing a sea kayaking business. Maxi had his own chair in the office but if he felt ignored he would try to pull Fi out of her chair to gain her attention. He became the kayak base puppy and all the guides loved him. Within a short time he had inserted himself in their pre-departure safety talk, and would often swim out to the kayaks as the paddlers went through the capsize drill.

He also 'helped' at the end of each day, following the guides around as they cleaned gear and stacked the kayaks. The smell of salt and sweat on the guides seemed to mesmerise Maxi and he loved to lick them, with a look of adoration on his hairy face. He learnt to go kayaking with Fi, and even went surfing with her on the south coast. If he was left behind on the beach he would run out to join her as she surfed towards the shore.

Brian usually took Maxi to the vet, as he had better control over him, but a rather embarrassing event took place once when Fi had to take him to the vet for a blood test when Brian was away. Maxi, although a big rangy dog, was very nervous about being in the small examination room with Mike, the tall vet. He knew what was coming and his heart rate went up when he saw the needle coming towards him. Instantly he started struggling, throwing his long legs around the examination table, his big paws slipping on the stainless steel. The more Mike tried to hold him, the more Maxi fought to get off the table and out the door.

Everything went seriously wrong when Maxi thrust himself backwards into the wall, saliva flying everywhere, and knocked over a rack of pamphlets. Mike, who was by now quite cross, decided that the blood test was not a happening thing, so Fi left the examination room, dragging Maxi behind her.

On the way through the reception, Maxi spotted a pile of new dog beds that had just been delivered. Going to the end of his lead he just managed to reach them, quickly cocked his leg and, with a look of total satisfaction, peed all over them. Poor Fi. She dragged Maxi through reception, calling out, 'Just put it all on the bill!'

While on a walk with Brian around the lake, Maxi decided to nobble a duck. A stranger who witnessed it happening called out to Brian, 'Not a good look, mate.' An embarrassed Brian gathered up the traumatised duck and headed home, Maxi slinking along beside him. He knew he was in trouble (again). Brian filled the small swimming pond in their back yard and thankfully, when he placed the duck in the water, it seemed okay. He then sat Maxi in the pond and ordered him to SIT and STAY while the duck swam around him. Looking very guilty and bedraggled, Maxi obeyed, his head hanging low, not daring to make eye contact with the duck.

My grandmother once said to me, 'Ruthie, you try to be good but you just can't.' Maxi makes me think of this.

However, when the duck had fully recovered, Brian took it back to the boat harbour, and Maxi never again nobbled a duck. Perhaps the old dog has learnt something.

Two months after I had started to write up Maxi's story he was diagnosed with bone cancer. He was the perfect patient: gobbled up his medication, limped around with his wagging tail still held high. But the tumour on his leg slowly got bigger, to the point where it was difficult for him to walk any further than the length of the garden. For a time, Brian and Fi took him for walks in the wheelbarrow to stimulate his mind.

Whenever I visited, Maxi showed his delight by actually smiling. Although there were many good days as he adapted to hopping about on his three good legs, the general trajectory was down for Maxi. Finally, on 20 July 2022, it was time to say goodbye. He was having a happy day, alert and full of himself when the vet arrived, and at 2.15 p.m. he took his last breath. Fi and Brian sat with him and wept, knowing they had made the right decision.

I am so grateful that he is in my book. The big, loping, joyful dog who loved everyone and was one of my bookshop dogs.

Stella, in the previous story, was Maxi's best friend. They went on holidays together, spending weeks down in Riverton, and although Maxi was much bigger, weighing in at 30 kilograms, he often let her win a play-fight. He was like her big brother.

Stella has now lost her best friend and playmate.

Rafferty

RAFFERTY THE GENTLE GIANT

A Toyota Wish people-mover pulled up just along from the Wee Bookshops. As frequently happens, a dog started barking in the vehicle as soon the couple got out and walked towards the bookshops.

'We're dog friendly so your dog can come out and join us if you like,' I said after we had introduced ourselves.

The couple just smiled. Mike told me his dog was *very large* and it may not be a good idea to have him around the bookshops, but would I like to meet him? Of course I would. All I could see through the back window was the top of four hairy legs and a long shaggy body. Maybe a Shetland pony? That would be a first for the bookshops.

We crossed to the car and Mike came and stood beside me. 'Want me to let him out?'

'That would be brilliant.'

He opened the back and there stood a magnificent Irish wolfhound with soft enquiring eyes and body indicating great eagerness to get out of the vehicle. Mike attached a thick lead with a large carabiner clip to the dog's wide leather collar. 'Out you get, Rafferty.'

It was instant love. I gave him a huge hug and he leaned in to me. 'How much does he weigh?' I asked Mike.

'Rafferty weighs between 72 and 75 kilos,' he replied. 'I'm not sure exactly, because I can no longer lift him onto the scales and he refuses to cooperate when we visit the vet.'

That's a lot of dog.

'I'm also unsure of his height but he's about 86 centimetres. Dog height is measured to the shoulder when standing on all four paws.'

Mike looked small with Rafferty standing quietly beside him, head held high, looking proud and confident.

The Irish wolfhound is a 'sighthound', which hunts by visual perception alone, and they were once used to pursue game at speed. They were also used as a guard dog, specialising in protection against — and the hunting of — wolves. They were not always successful as guard dogs, because although they're huge and that may seem intimidating, they are often friendly towards strangers. By nature they are loyal, affectionate and devoted, and certainly fearless if they or their family are facing danger.

In 1902 the Irish wolfhound was declared the regimental mascot of the Irish Guards. When poet W.B. Yeats was looking for potent symbols to stir the Irish to recall their mythical past, he chose the shamrock, the harp and the Irish wolfhound.

Mike and Lorna are certainly keen on the breed because Rafferty is their *third* Irish wolfhound. Mike liked the breed after first meeting one as a child. A family living near him was visited by their eldest son who brought along his Irish wolfhound named Finn. Finn roamed the neighbourhood and occasionally came onto Mike's family property.

Mack, their own small dog, would charge at Finn, barking ferociously — but from a safe distance. On one occasion Finn took Mack by the scruff of the neck, gently tossed him to one side, then crouched low, wagging his tail, apparently hoping the game would continue. Mike was so impressed by the big dog's good nature that he decided he wanted one when he was older.

When they brought Rafferty home from the breeder's he was two months old and weighed 9.5 kg. It was a long drive home from Canterbury and the puppy cried most of the way. Mike slept on the floor with him for the first few nights, cuddling him to give him company and warmth. After a short time he settled down, and doubled his weight in the first month.

'We wanted to give him an Irish name,' Mike told me, 'and preferably one that wasn't used too often. Rafferty is a name with origins in Ulster (Northern Ireland) and it caught our attention by being the last name of the singer/ songwriter Gerry Rafferty.'

Rafferty, like so many puppies, developed a fetish for socks and would steal them, even though he knew he wasn't supposed to. He would hide them in his mouth and dash outside to bury them in the garden. Thankfully he grew out of this fetish. He has swallowed a couple of birds, one of them a sparrow he caught when it flew into their house. Lorna called Mike at work in great distress as she heard it cheeping as it went down Rafferty's throat. The other was a duckling that came onto their property with its mother and siblings.

I could tell Mike loved talking about his wolfhound, who is now three and a half years old. They were a team of two, standing smiling (yes, Rafferty was smiling) as they leaned in to each other on the side of the road.

'What is it like owning such a massive dog?' I asked.

'Irish wolfhounds are friendly, with a calm, placid temperament most of the time,' Mike replied. 'But their size would be a problem for anyone who didn't have a large, well-fenced property, or who was unable to exercise their dog. Wolfhounds are not hyperactive but they need a good run a few times a week.'

He smiled. 'We live in a very small house and chaos ensues if Rafferty is bored and becomes boisterous. It's easy for him to accidentally knock someone over by just turning around. Dining tables, coffee tables and benches cease to be safe places to put down food when you have an Irish wolfhound in the home, as everything is at the dog's eye level. It's common to find a hairy hound nose under your armpit when you're preparing food.'

And how do other people react?

'Potential owners should be prepared for the reactions they may get when in public. These range from joy to astonished interest, to fear and hostility from people who see a large monster, rather than a friendly dog wagging its tail.'

Despite his size, Rafferty apparently doesn't eat that much, but he ate voraciously as a puppy while he was growing. Just like any other affectionate dog he loves being patted, stroked, tickled behind the ears and having his belly scratched. If he's getting no attention he'll cry and roll on his back until someone obliges.

He has a great trick of sitting on your knee with his front paws on the floor, which gives visitors quite a surprise. He insists on meeting everyone, and any dog he encounters is boisterously welcomed. There is a beach, a river and a wetland near their home in Waikouaiti where they often go walking. Rafferty loves the beach but he's not interested in swimming and only goes into the sea or the river on a hot day to cool down.

Most of the locals know him as a friendly giant.

Mike went and sat in the doorway to the Children's Bookshop, while Lorna and their daughter explored the books. Rafferty was right behind him, ready for another cuddle.

Gracie

DOG-SITTING GRACIE

It was a sunny Fiordland afternoon when the SUV pulled up at the bookshops. A middle-aged couple came to wander around the three shops, introducing themselves as Andrew and Gaelynn from Christchurch. Our conversation flowed easily.

They were on a South Island tour and as they had never been to Manapōuri before, the Wee Bookshops were on their 'things to do' list. Before long Gaelynn asked if I knew where they could leave Gracie, their black labrador, for a day, as they wanted to go into Milford Sound. Gracie was sitting so quietly in the rear of the vehicle I hadn't even realised they had a dog with them.

'We love dogs — let her out so we can meet.'

Gaelynn let Gracie out of the back of the vehicle where she had been curled up on a cosy bed. She was pure black, with trusting brown eyes and beautiful big paws. I dropped down to her level and talked to her, all the time patting her and scratching behind her ears. She was soft and calm, quietly checking me out.

Without hesitation I offered to have Gracie for the day. I told them that our very large back yard was fully fenced and a perfect playground for dogs — as long as they would accept sharing the space with our chickens! Our four hens range all day in the forest we have planted behind our home.

Gaelynn was delighted. I ran in to get Lance. 'You have to come and meet a dog named Gracie,' I babbled. 'Can we look after her tomorrow?'

With a sense of slight resignation Lance came over to the bookshop with me and met Gracie and her owners. We showed them our back yard, explained that we were used to dogs and in fact had Cove staying with us at the time.

We chatted for a long time and discovered that Gaelynn owned the pet crematorium Loving Tributes, near Lincoln, just outside Christchurch. The way she spoke about it confirmed that she was gentle and compassionate — just the sort of person you would want beside you when saying goodbye to your beloved companion.

And that was how Gracie came to stay at our place for the day.

Early the next day they dropped her off. Gracie looked a bit wistful as she watched her owners drive away. We played with her in the back yard, and sat and talked to her until we felt she was settled enough to be left by herself. Cove in his dotage had decided that the best way to accommodate his visitor was to totally ignore her, as long as she didn't sit on his bed or steal his toy rabbit.

Gracie kept herself busy exploring, chewing on a bone and lying in the sunshine. We kept popping out to check on her and she appeared to be happy. Then, when I came back from the bookshops to have lunch with Lance, we heard a soulful cry that sounded like a wolf howl! When I was in Germany I went to a wolf reserve and heard the wolves calling at dusk. I had never heard anything so full of sadness — it was as though they were seeking our understanding.

I looked out the window and saw Gracie sitting straight and tall, holding her head high, looking up at the sky exactly like a wolf — and howling. We rushed out to her and I wrapped my arms around her. She snuggled in to me.

'Looks like she'll be inside with us for the rest of the day,' said Lance.

Gaelynn and Andrew returned late afternoon, having had a wonderful day in Milford Sound, and Gracie was overjoyed to see them. We sat and had a coffee, chatting about the day, and then said our goodbyes.

Several months later, when I had decided to write this book, I got in touch with them. They were delighted to be included, and we arranged to have a Zoom meeting as I had so many questions. Plus I wanted to see Gracie.

I was particularly interested in Gaelynn's pet crematorium. She said she came up with the idea because of her love of animals. She had been trained as a counsellor and as her great-grandfather had been a funeral director it may have been in her blood. She was only 22 when their baby daughter, Melissa, died from congenital heart defects. Having experienced that deep sense of loss, Gaelynn decided to open a pet crematorium and offer grief support.

Setting it up had been a long, stressful and expensive process, but Gaelynn was determined and got there in the end. A small log cottage in the peaceful 8000-square-metre garden is the perfect reception area. Out at the back of the log cabin is the actual crematorium, which the manufacturers taught Gaelynn how to operate.

She visited the SPCA and offered to cremate — at no cost — any pets that had to be put down because they had no owner. Rather than having them end up in a landfill, this was how she honoured their lives, and also how she perfected her skills. Every wee animal deserved a respectful farewell.

'The other side of grief is love,' Gaelynn told me. 'I allow time for pet owners to talk about whatever they want. We share their stories, speak about the life of their pet, their companionship and the ultimate love connection. The strength of love in their relationship is so important and it is up to me to honour that relationship.'

Each pet is cremated individually, never with another animal, and the ashes are returned to the owners in an engraved container.

At the end of our second Zoom meeting we gave each

other a virtual hug. Gracie had been in and nestled her head on Gaelynn's knee, so she was given a virtual hug as well.

We both cried, not just because of our special friendship, but for all the pets that help shape our lives — the ability of dogs to forgive, their constant loyalty and unconditional love, and their incredible insight into how we feel. Every one of them deserves to be honoured and remembered.

I thank them all for being such a special part of my book.

ACKNOWLEDGEMENTS

There she sat — a wee, tidy, shiny bundle, silent, waiting. I hadn't seen her for nearly three months, but she was back again. As I approached my bookshops she looked across at me, her tail wagging in a silent welcome.

'Hello,' I said, quietly, as I sat down beside her. 'Where have you been?' I touched her small head and let my hand slide gently down her back; she snuggled in closer to me.

'Nice to have you visit again. I have written a book about the dogs that visit my bookshop, and sadly, you are not in it as I haven't seen you for so long.'

I opened the bookshop, picked a dog treat from the bag and gave it to her. She took it from my hand very gently, looked up at me with enquiring eyes, then left with the small gift held in her mouth. This was the fourth time she had visited over the past three years. I don't even know her name.

Later in the day, Stu walked past with his Weight Watchers champion of the year, Kane. He also didn't make the book as I didn't get to know him until the manuscript was finished. He has lost nearly 10 kilos under the care and management of Stu, who adopted him from the SPCA.

I love every dog that comes to my bookshops, and I thank them for being the stars in my book.

I remember Hunza. Just his name brings me to tears.

To all the owners, thank you for your patience and for sharing your dog stories with me. Dogs are the champions of unconditional love, displaying extreme patience and understanding and placing total trust in those who care for them. The owners in this book were washed with the same brush, lessons learnt from their best friends, their dogs.

Dainty, your sense of humour and understanding with every dog you met while writing this book was incredible. You never let me down. 'There is a huge dog here at the bookshop that looks like a black bear. He must be in my book! Can you drop everything and come over?' And you would, camera in hand, accompanied by your faithful partner, Shady Lady.

To Lance, my soulmate and best friend. Not only has he put up with the many piles of books sitting quietly throughout our home, but during the writing of this book, he had a continual flow of dog owners dropping in for coffee before, during and after their dog's photoshoot.

To everyone at Allen & Unwin, I am so proud to be one of your authors. Thank you for supporting my idea of writing a book about the dogs that visit my bookshops. Thank you for your incredible support, advice, and belief in me. Jenny Hellen, who has stood by me, who is so gentle when giving advice and who has incredible insight. Rachel, my editor, thank you again for all the time you dedicate to checking every sentence, your subtle suggestions, and your kindness — it means a lot to me. I am extremely grateful that my book is in the safe hands of Saskia Nicol — the amazing designer of my previous book, *The Bookseller at the End of the World*. Also to Sophie Watson, illustrator, thank you for your ideas and talent. And of course, Abba, who keeps me on track, promotes me with incredible enthusiasm and answers the many stupid questions I ask with concern and understanding.

Not to be forgotten, Sandra, Rights and International Sales Manager — what a star!

Finally, to my readers, the cornerstone of all books. Without readers, our books would not find homes, the book would never be opened, the pages never touched. I sincerely hope one or more of the dogs' stories touches your heart, and makes you cry and laugh. Thank you for giving my book a home at your place.

Ruth

ABOUT THE AUTHOR

Ruth Shaw runs a cluster of wee bookshops in remote
Manapōuri in the far south of New Zealand. She lives
on-site with her husband, Lance. In 2022 she published her
first memoir, *The Bookseller at the End of the World*, a book
that has since become a critically acclaimed national and
international treasure. Ruth's book has been translated
into Italian, Dutch, German, Turkish and Chinese.

If you love this book, try Ruth Shaw's first book *The Bookseller at the End of the World*.